CW00500382

Volker Kratzenberg-Annies

A   J O U R N E Y   O F   D I S C O V E R Y

In cooperation with the European Space Agency

Harry N. Abrams, INC., Publishers

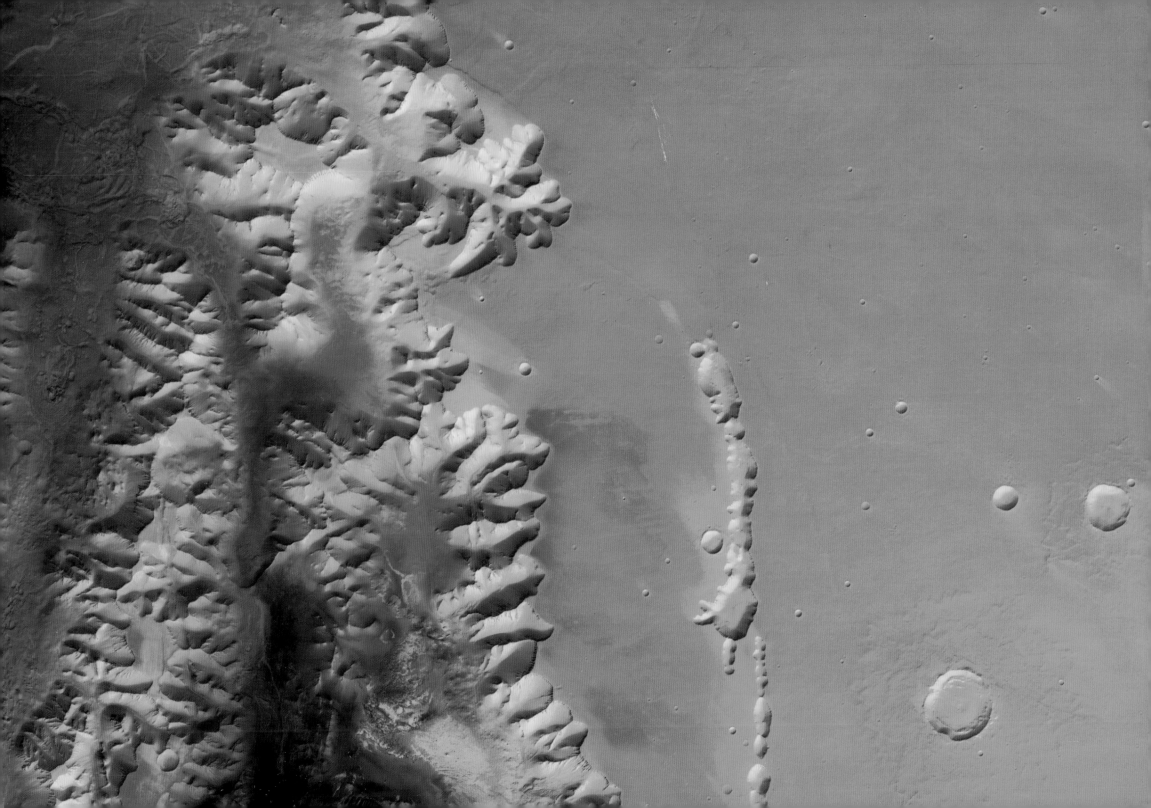

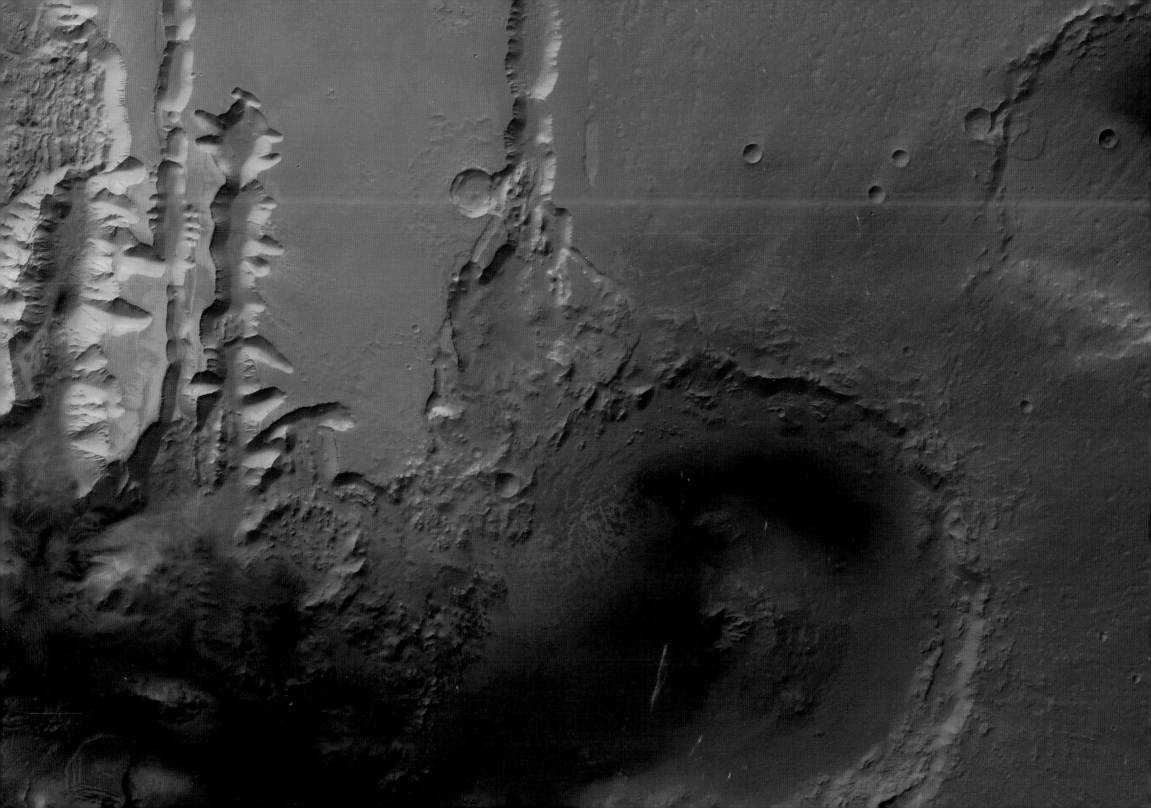

Images on these pages

Front cover: the Pleiades, as "seen," by the Hubble Space Telescope.

Pages 2/3: Martian landscape photographed by Mars Express.

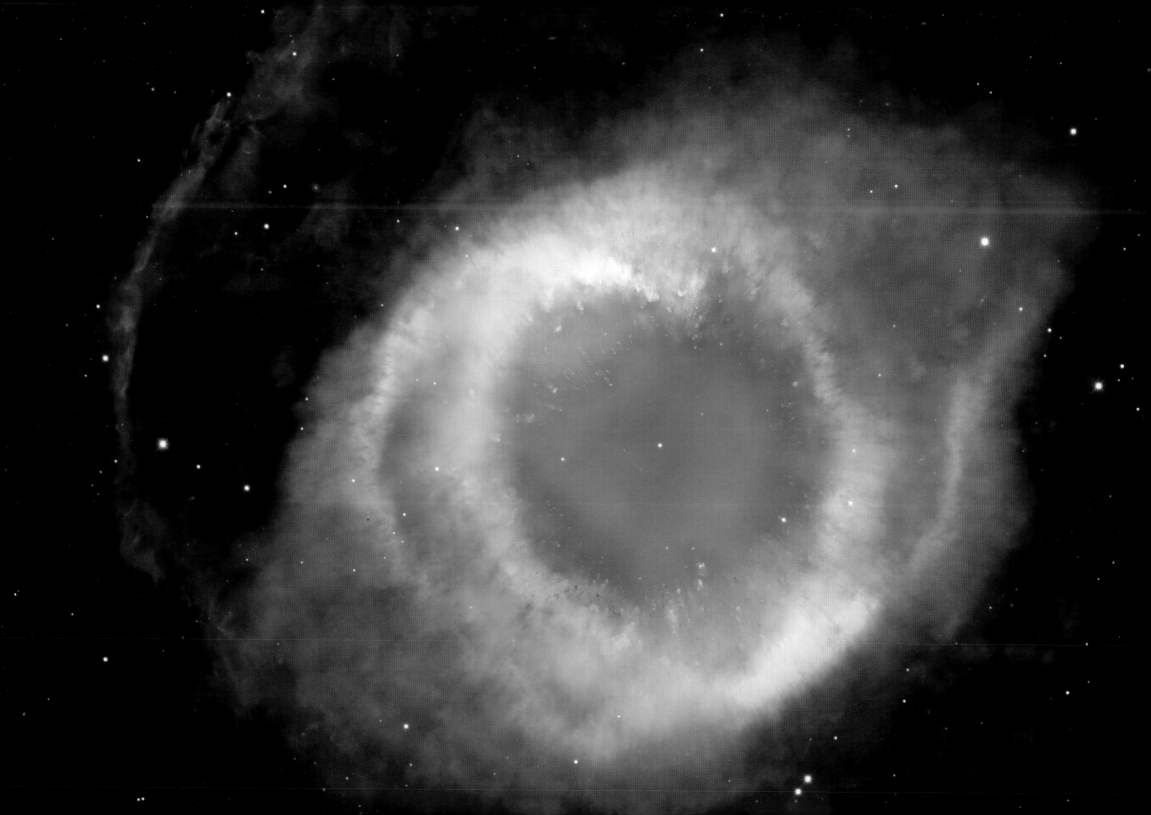

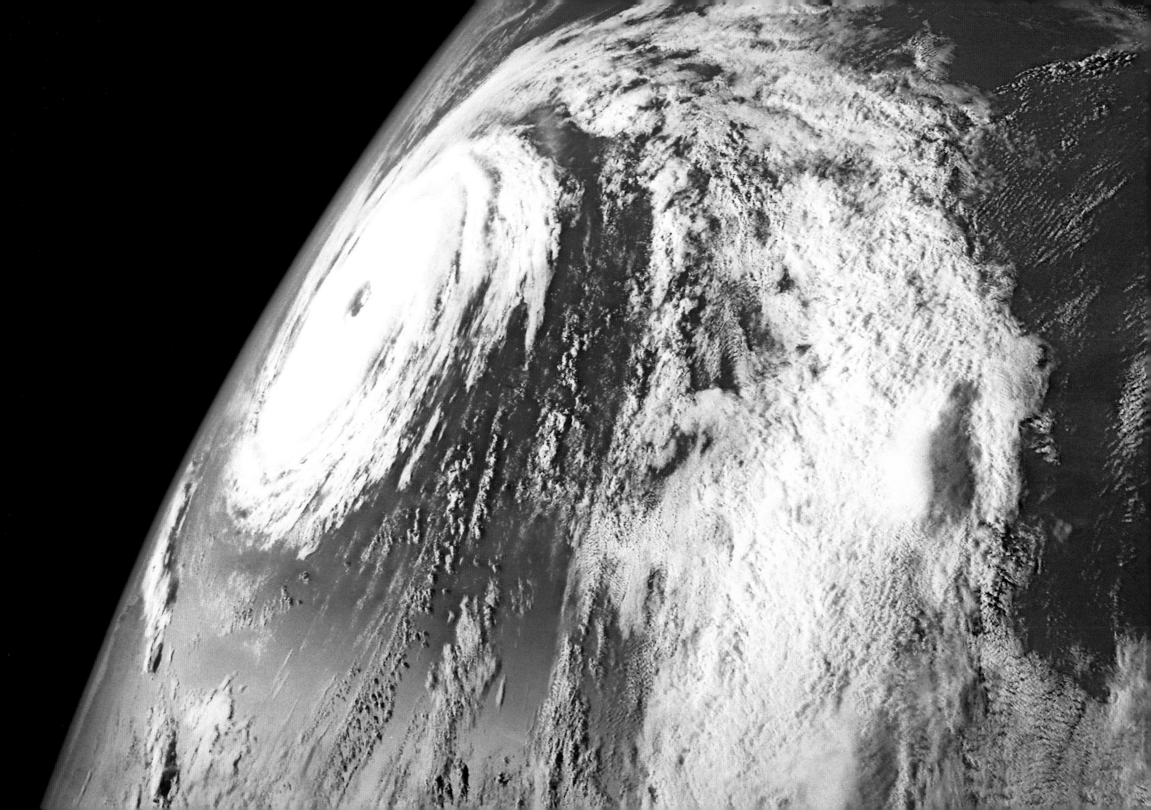

CONTENTS

FOREWORD

For some time now, space has formed part of our daily lives. Never a day goes by in which we do not, in one way or another, benefit from applications, such as weather forecasting, satellite navigation and live television broadcasts, which are either reliant on space activities or are spin-offs from them. In addition, Earth observation by satellite is a vital tool for research into our environment.

Yet that is not all: space also exerts a powerful fascination, largely due to the efforts to explore it by astronaut or automatic probe. The exploration of unknown worlds within our Solar System; the observation of distant stars and galaxies beyond the Milky Way; the search for extra-terrestrial life and the quest for the origins of the universe. These are all matters of more than mere scientific interest. And the more we gaze out into space, the more we learn about our own planet, about its origins and development, and our place in the cosmos; in other words, where we have come from and where we are going.

Thus, if all space activities have one thing in common, it is that they enrich our lives, whether it be through technological innovation or by giving rise to inspirational discoveries and new insights.

In this book, you are invited to plunge into the fascinating world of space and witness breathtaking images of moons, planets, stars and galaxies, photographs taken by astronauts on space flights as well as some of the most impressive satellite images of the Earth, which are dedicated to preserving the natural conditions on which life on our home planet depends.

11

Left: The first requirement for all space exploration and, by extension, a great many achievements and discoveries, is rockets powerful enough to carry heavy loads into space. Europe's Ariane 5 in Kourou, French Guiana shortly before launch.

STUDYING THE ENVIRONMENT FROM SPACE

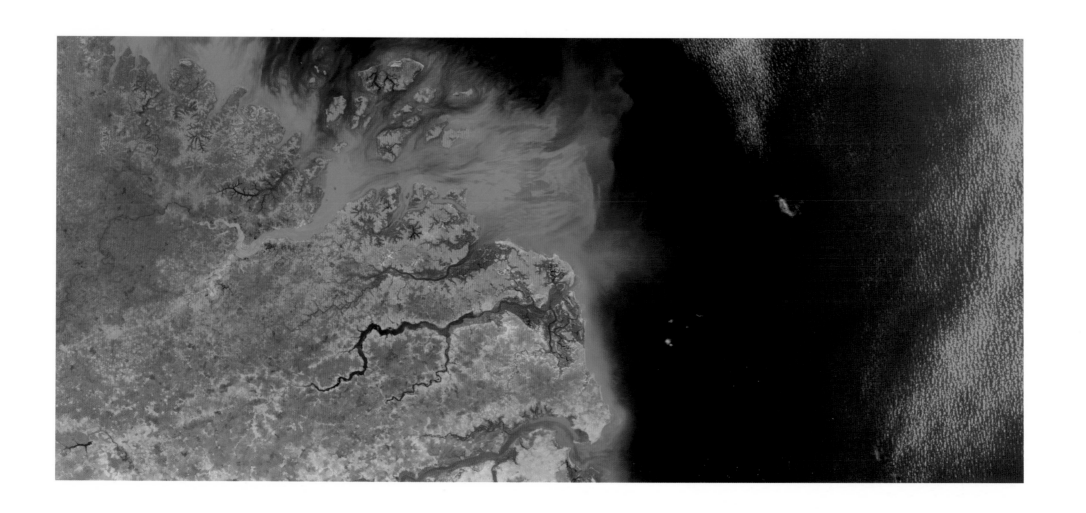

STUDYING THE ENVIRONMENT FROM SPACE

No sooner were human beings in a position to fly off into space than they began to cast their eyes back in wonder at their home planet. Soon after, the first satellites were launched, making Earth observation possible. Therefore, much of space activity until the present day could essentially be described as a "mission to planet Earth".

Many environmental questions can only be answered by observing the Earth as a whole. Orbiting satellites collect data on climatic events around the clock, documenting and analysing ecologically significant changes to seas and continents.

The biggest and most sophisticated environmental satellite ever built, Envisat (see small picture, right), was developed by ESA, the European Space Agency. It is capable of observing the Earth's surface using radar sensors, even through cloud – as is essential for studying the rain forest for example – and can also produce images by night. Each day, Envisat transmits the latest data on the condition of the ozone layer, and thousands of scientists from all around the world use its data to gain a better understanding of the Earth's ecosystem. This in turn enables them to make recommendations on how to achieve a responsible and sustainable environmental policy.

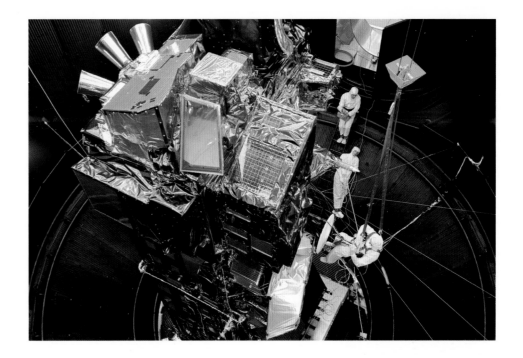

15

The following pages show a selection of images from this and other satellites, which aim to provide an overview of the broad spectrum covered by Earth observation and its applications. False colours are often used in the processing of such satellite images to highlight key information.

Left: the coast of West Africa with Guinea Bissau to the south of Senegal. In this false-colour image from Europe's Envisat environmental satellite, vegetation stands out in reddish tones. The water in the coastal area clouded by river sediment is clearly visible in green.

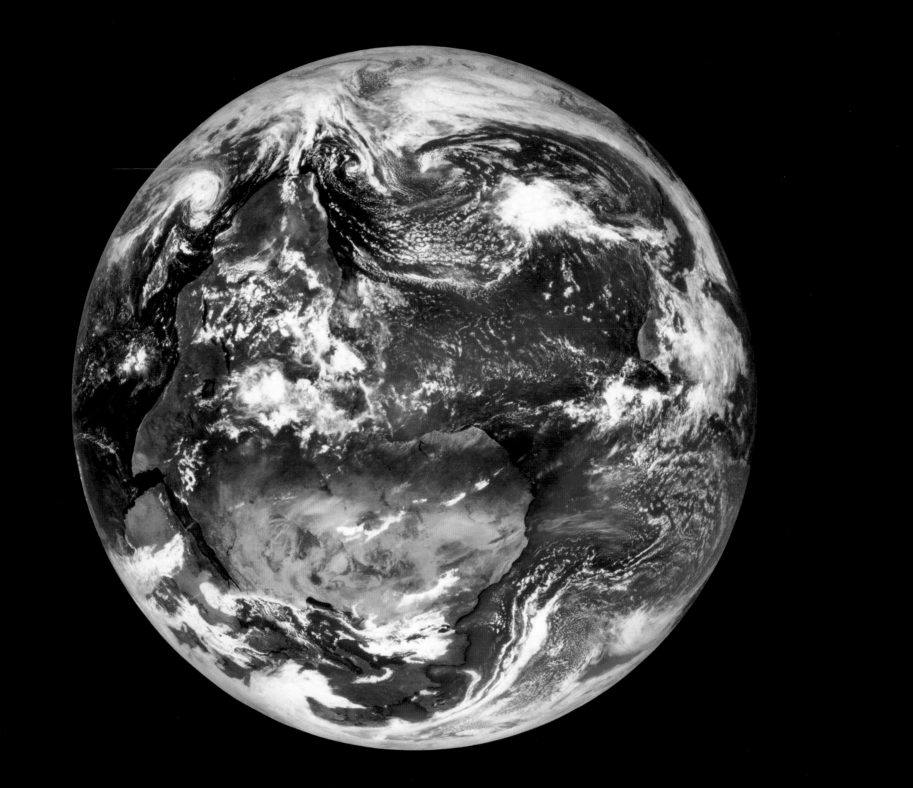

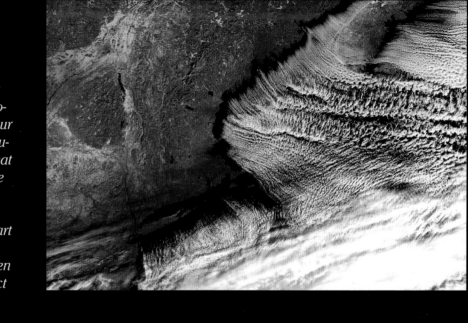

The Earth, or to be more precise, its western hemisphere, as seen by Europe's Meteosat 2 weather satellite from a distance of 36,000 kilometres. At that distance, it takes satellites exactly 24 hours to orbit our planet. Because the Earth takes the same time to perform one revolution, the satellite appears to remain above the same spot. This is what is known as a "geostationary" orbit. Its advantage is that the satellite always shows the same area on the Earth's surface. In this way, it is possible to gather precise data for weather forecasting. Indeed, the accuracy of this data has continually improved in recent years, in part due to constant refinements in satellite technology. Whereas in the past, meteorologists were liable to make the occasional mistake even when forecasting the next day's weather, it is now possible to predict developments in the weather for the whole week ahead with ever increasing accuracy. This is not just of benefit to us when planning what to do with our free time, but is also extremely important in many professional domains (air transport, shipping and agriculture to name but a few).

WHEN SATELLITES SAVE LIVES

Each year, thousands of lives are saved thanks to sophisticated satellite technology. These "sentries" out in space spot the first signs of hurricanes forming far out at sea. Before the advent of satellites, however, they would often remain undiscovered in their early stages. Now it is possible to accurately determine the strength, speed and direction of a hurricane or typhoon, thus providing populations with advance warning so that in an emergency they can be called upon to evacuate threatened regions.

Left: this image taken by Meteosat 8, one of the most up-to-date weather satellites in the world, shows Hurricane Ivan as it races towards the coast of the United States (image by EUMETSAT).

Above right: Hurricane Isabel approaching America's Atlantic coast. This image taken by Envisat in September 2003 uses false colours to show the surface temperature of clouds and thus their altitude.
Below right: this "multitemporal" image by NASA is so called because it combines three satellite images of the same hurricane taken at different times. It thus shows the hurricane growing in size as it approaches the coast of the United States.

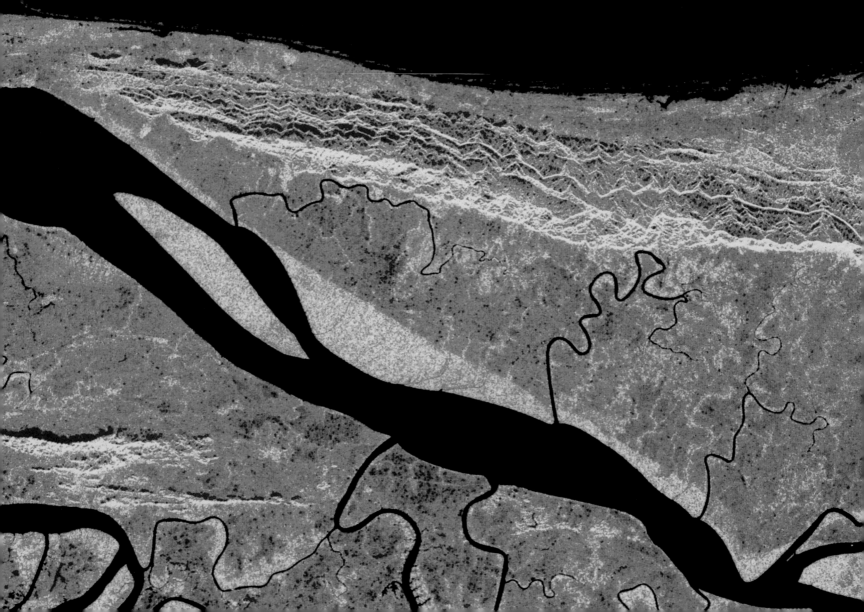

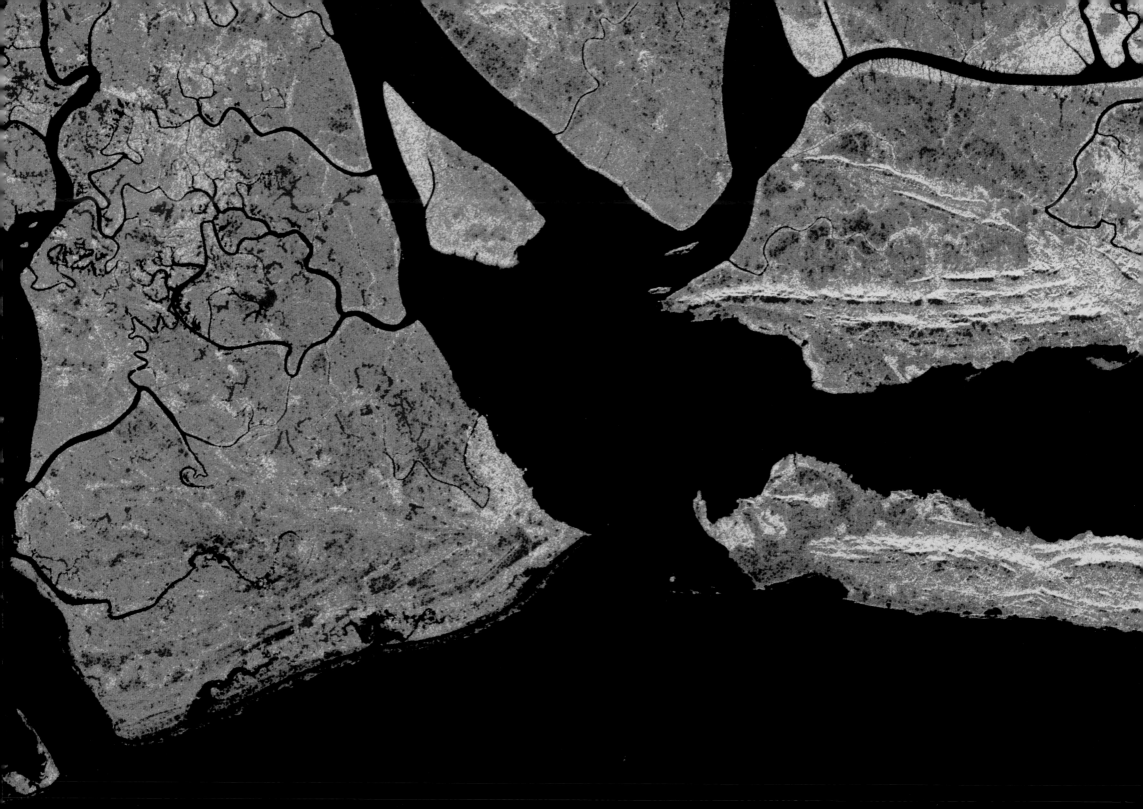

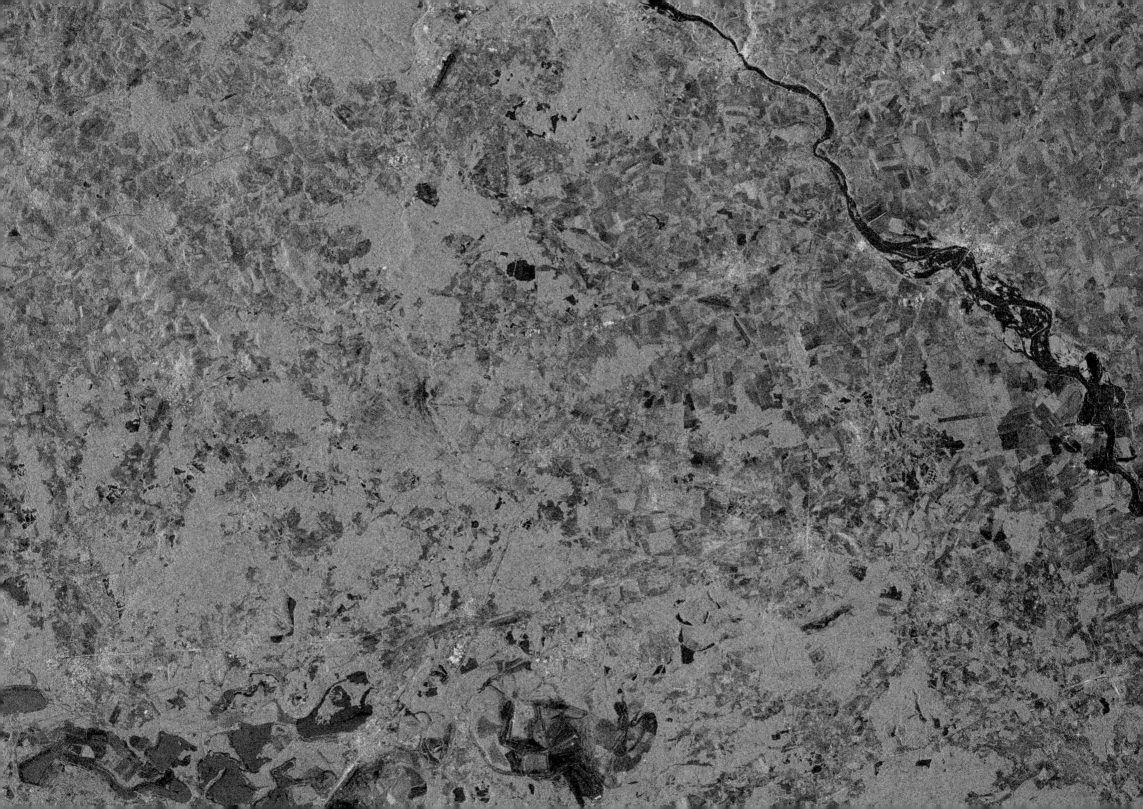

BEFORE THE FLOOD

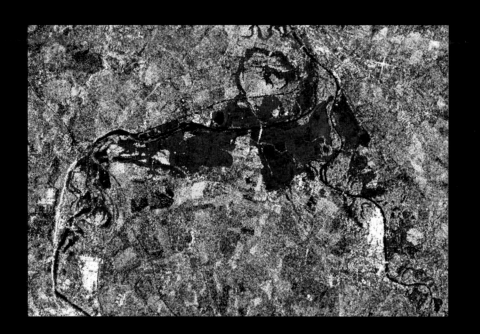

The image on pages 22 and 23 shows the coastal region of Myanmar (formerly Burma). With much of the country barely above sea level, flooding is a particularly frequent occurrence. The image is from the joint US-German SRTM shuttle mission tasked with creating a 3D digital map of the Earth.

In recent years, Europe too has seen rivers such as the Rhone, Rhine and Elbe break their banks with increasing frequency. With the aid of satellite images, areas threatened by flooding can be identified early and local authorities can take precautions before the next flood occurs. These images taken by Envisat in August 2002 show the Elbe in Germany (left) and in the vicinity of Prague (right). Flood zones are shown in blue.

Following pages, left: *the Lena Delta in Russia (false-colour image by Landsat 7).*
Following pages, right: *the Maldives, one of the threatened paradises of the Earth, photographed by the Terra satellite.*

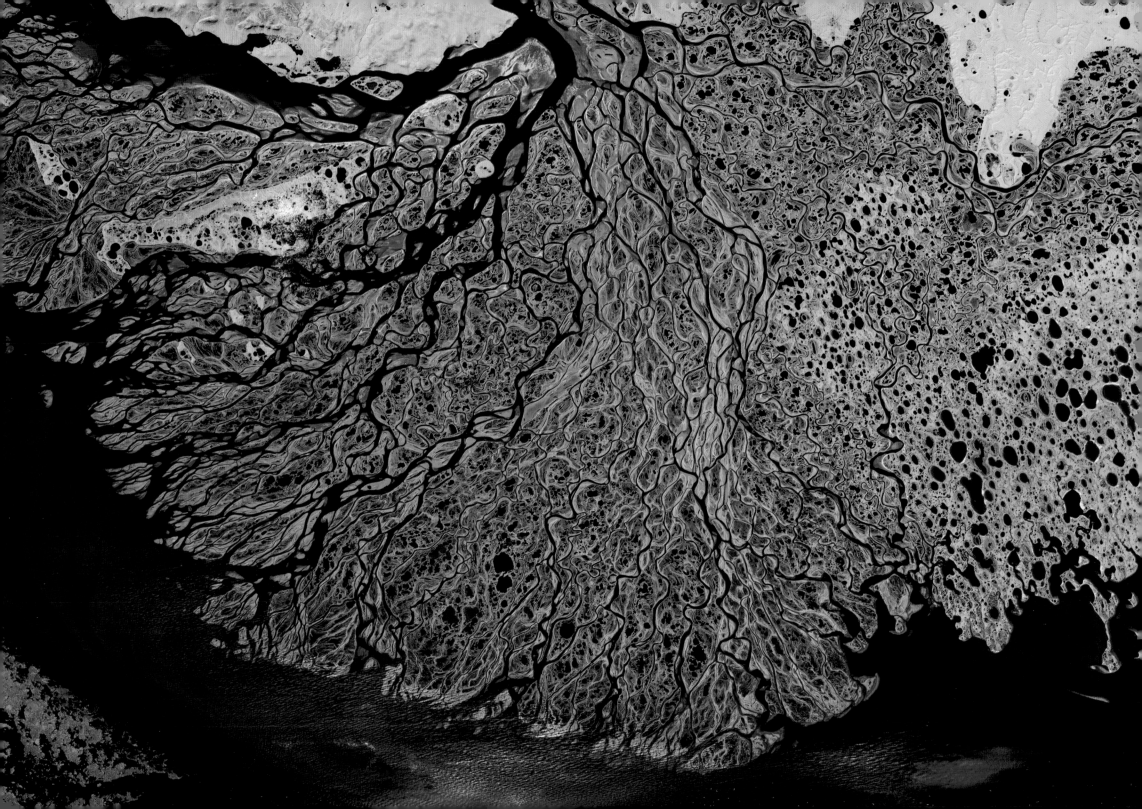

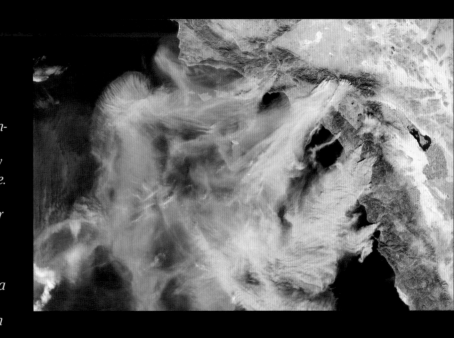

The South of France is regularly affected by severe forest fires. The main photograph (left) shows the plume of smoke from a fire still burning to the right of the picture by the coast and further to the left, grey areas which are already burnt out. Satellite images help emergency services with their planning and enable them to provide rapid assistance.

Information gathered from space is also helpful in other areas of disaster prevention and crisis management: when earthquakes occur, satellite images provide initial assessments of the extent of the damage and show which roads remain passable by rescue teams. When events such as flooding, volcanic eruptions and landslides occur, satellite data is often required to assist with prevention or with rescue efforts. Therefore, the European Space Agency, ESA, has, along with the French space agency, CNES, the Canadian Space Agency and other partners, put in place a system to immediately provide the responsible authorities with all available satellite data in the event of an emergency. The UN is also part of this disaster prevention network.

A HELPING HAND FOR FARMERS

From a great height, farming land can look just like a patchwork quilt. The image of Rotterdam to the left taken by France's SPOT 4 satellite (Copyright CNES 1999. Distribution: Spot Image) and that of the Netherlands on the right, recorded by ESA's Envisat satellite, use false colours to reveal vast amounts of information. The type of detailed data such false-colour images provide varies according to the sensors and data processing methods used. Thus, individual shades can be attributed to the various plant types growing in particular fields. In addition, the ripeness of cereals, rice and other crops can be determined and assessed in an instant from the several hundred kilometre high orbit. Thus, farmers too benefit from information gathered in space. Such data is also of use to the authorities, for example to monitor whether land purported to be set aside for which farmers receive subsidies is in fact left uncultivated.

WHEN THE EARTH MOVES UNDER OUR FEET

Images provided by satellite have long been an indispensable tool for town planners, who may draw on data gathered from space for many different purposes, such as designating construction zones, planning road layouts and ascertaining the impact of large-scale construction projects on a town's microclimate. One of the most common applications is measuring subsidence, caused, for instance, by the construction of new subway lines. Indeed, it is satellites which are best suited to measuring changes in elevation thanks to the extraordinary precision of their instruments, and they can do so to the nearest millimetre despite orbiting at an altitude of over 800 kilometres.

Rises in ground elevation caused by natural phenomena, such as imminent volcanic eruptions, can also be detected in this way. For such purposes, satellite data form an important part of the early warning system.

Left: *radar image of Paris. It is mainly radar sensors which are used to determine changes in elevation.*

Above right: *Venice and the Grand Canal, where sinking ground levels are monitored particularly closely.*
Below right: *Mount Etna, Sicily.*

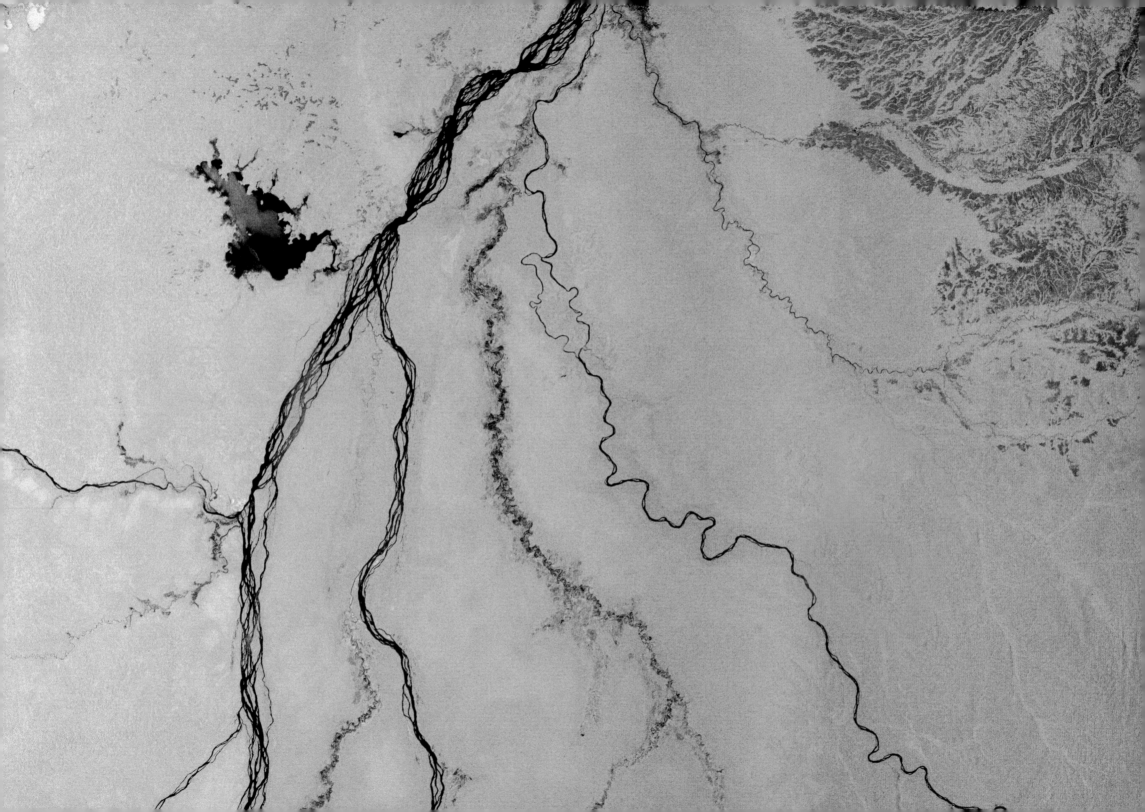

THE SEARCH FOR WATER

Water is a precious resource, especially in many parts of Africa. Its presence is not always easily detectable, as with large rivers (such as the Congo, left). Satellites which, using radar signals, can even see below the Earth's surface, are able to detect the presence of subterranean water to a depth of 20 metres.

Following pages, left: *southwest Libya. In the 1980's a major project was started in the region to extract and use ground water.*

Following pages, right: *Lake Tana is Ethiopia's largest stretch of water. These images were recorded by various sensors on Envisat, which carries a total of ten different instruments. These are used to observe and examine the Earth, its polar ice, seas and atmosphere.*

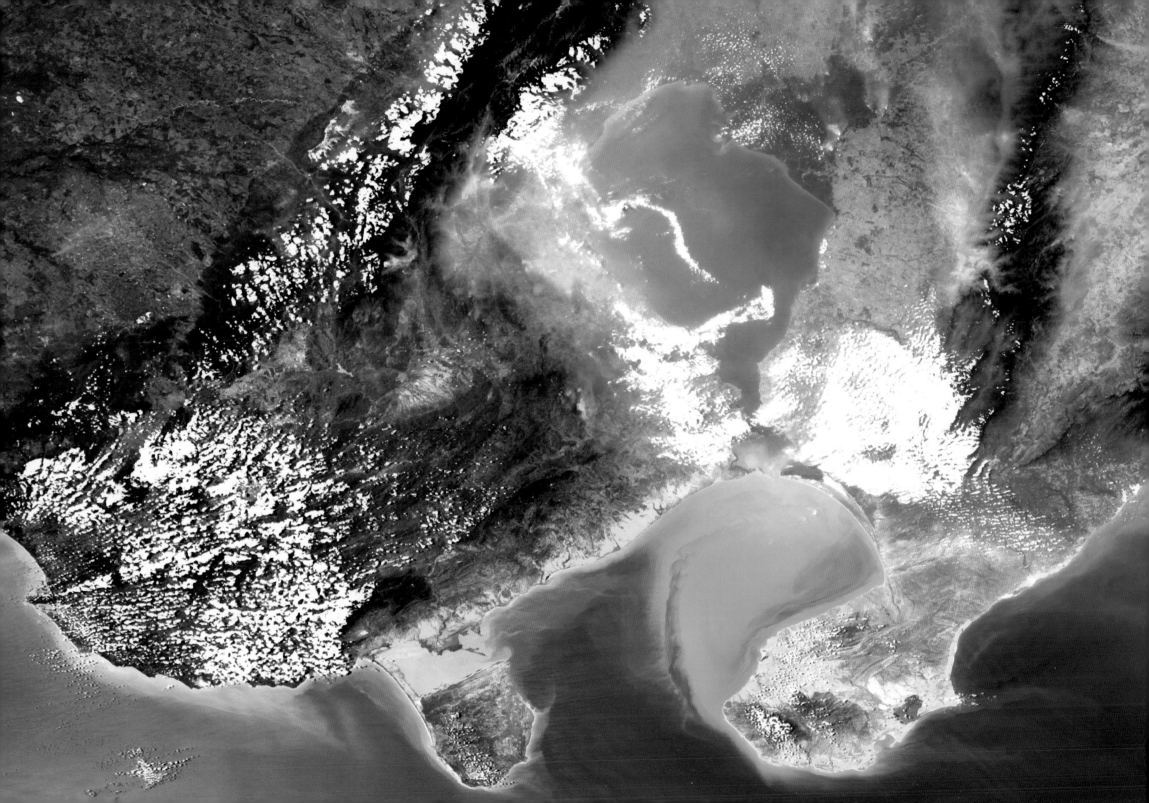

RAIN FORESTS ON FIRE

Northwest Venezuela: in the middle of the image in blue lies Lake Maracaibo, below the Guajira and Paraguaná peninsulas. Upon closer inspection, it is possible to observe smoke plumes produced by the burning rain forest. The great forests of South America have been described as the "green lung" of the Earth, and form a vital part of what might be characterised as our planet's "climate machine". Satellite images, therefore, serve both to monitor the clearing of tropical rain forests and reforestation. Thus, it is thanks to satellite monitoring that many international environmental protection treaties have become a reality.

SEAS RICH IN COLOUR

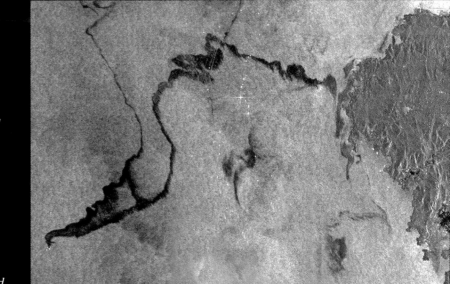

The Baltic Sea (left), with Finland to the North and Estonia to the South. Helsinki is visible in the top left corner of the picture. In this image, data recorded at various times by Envisat have been combined to form a composite image. Thus, experts are able to observe sea icing at various times of the year by using a range of false colours. In the Baltic States in particular, satellite data is assessed in this way to improve shipping safety.

It is also possible to use such data to trace ecological vandals who dump oil illicitly in the sea. Active radar instruments which "scan" the water surface are capable of positively identifying oil due to its very flat backscatter signal relative to water – such signals could be likened to an echo. This applies all the more when oil is discharged in large quantities following an accident, as occurred in November 2002 when the oil tanker Prestige foundered off the west coast of Spain. The picture above right shows oil trailing from the broken tanker.

Following pages, left: the English Channel, one of the busiest stretches of water in the world, showing the south of England and northern France. Unusually, this image shows north to the left instead of above. Following pages, right: the region around Archangel, Russia.

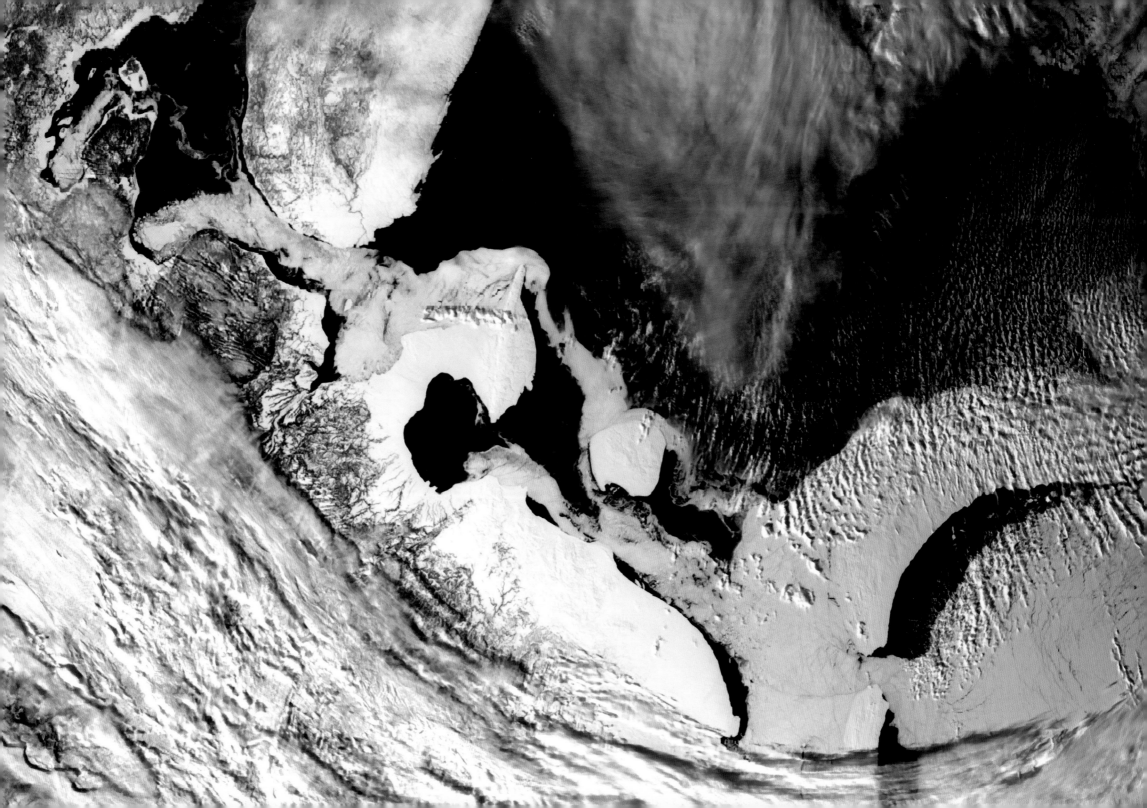

SURVEYING SNOW AND GLACIERS

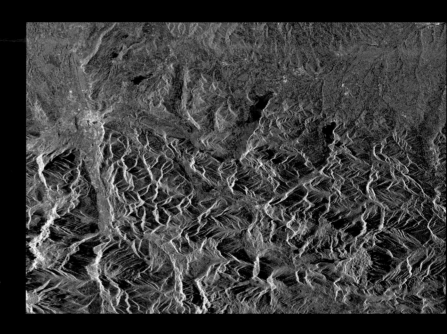

Northern Italy (left) with the Alps and the equally snow-capped peaks of the Apennines. Satellite images are used to study the consequences of climate change. Thus, for example, satellite data gathered over periods of several years and then compared are used to examine snow cover in the Alps and glacier shrinkage.

It is also possible to identify mountainsides threatened by erosion and areas at risk of avalanche. To that end, radar data are used to provide topographical information, notably on gradients.

Right: *the region around Salzburg, Austria. The town is in the top left of the picture.*

Following pages, left: *a glacier in Iceland (image by Landsat 7).*
Following pages, right: *the Alps and Lake Geneva.*

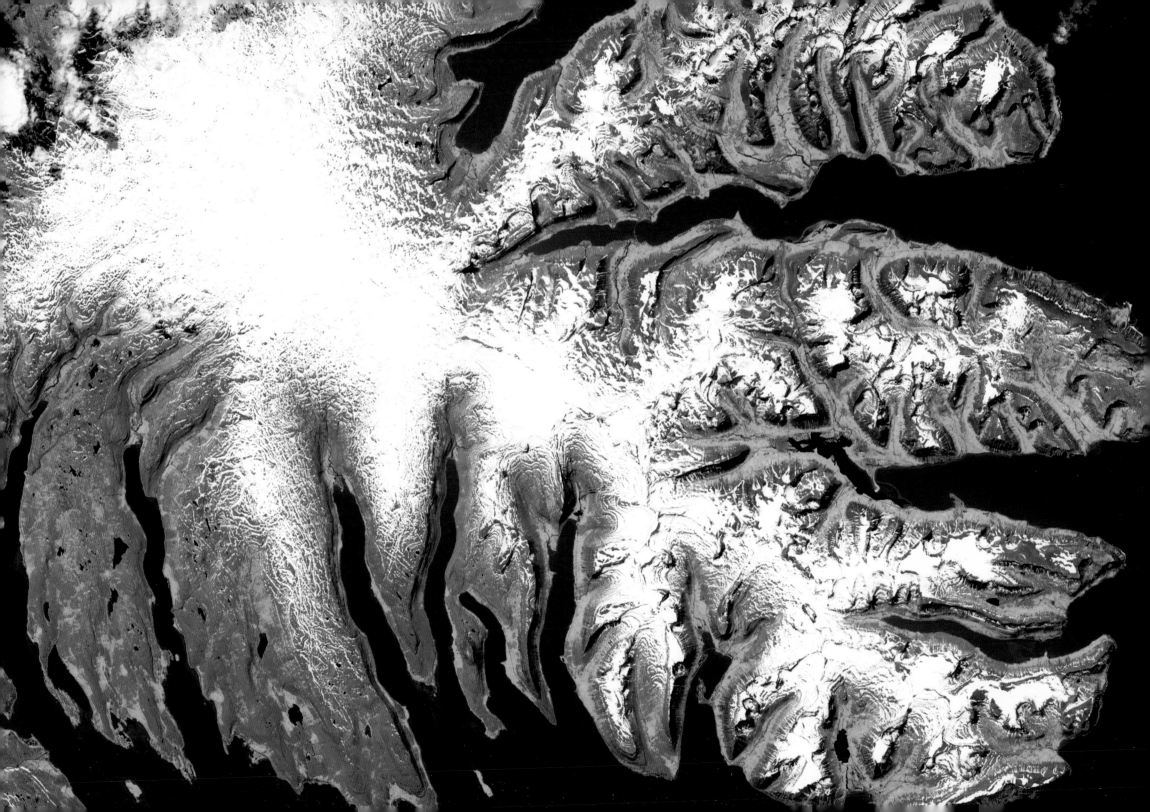

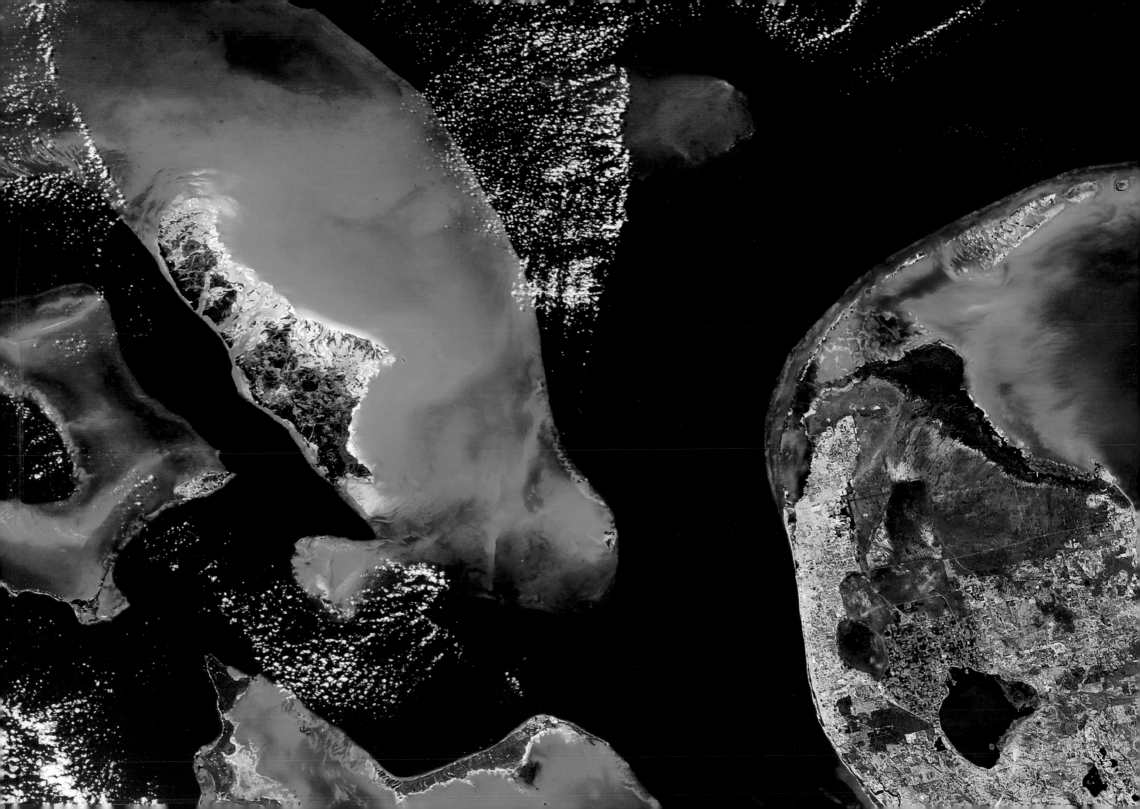

COULD THE GULF STREAM TURN TO A TRICKLE?

Oceans have a considerable influence on our climate. In addition to that, they serve as a source of food and are also frequently used for the disposal of waste. Despite the apparently endless expanses of water, the effects of human behaviour are clear to see. Moreover, climate change could transform ocean currents bringing serious consequences, which could even include the demise of the Gulf Stream, responsible for western Europe's moderate temperatures. Such an outcome cannot be entirely discounted and would have a lasting effect on the climate.

49

Satellites use a range of methods to examine the oceans, calculating, for example, the heights of waves and measuring ocean currents. Even sea temperatures can be accurately recorded to within a fraction of a degree.

Left: *the Caribbean (Florida and the Bahamas).*

Following pages: *Cuba, as seen by Envisat.*

IS THE ICE MELTING?

Global warming caused by the greenhouse effect is one of the most menacing environmental problems of our time. If we want to slow this process down or even one day bring it to a halt, it is crucial that we first gain a better understanding of the world's complex ecosystem. Only with accurate data can meaningful climate models be drawn up and effective counter-measures introduced. To that end, space has a unique contribution to make. As they orbit the Earth, satellites also gather a certain amount of information from inaccessible regions. Both of the pictures on these pages are of the Antarctic. The picture to the right, taken there in spring 2002, shows icebergs and ice floes up to 100 kilometres in length breaking away from the polar ice mass and drifting out to sea.

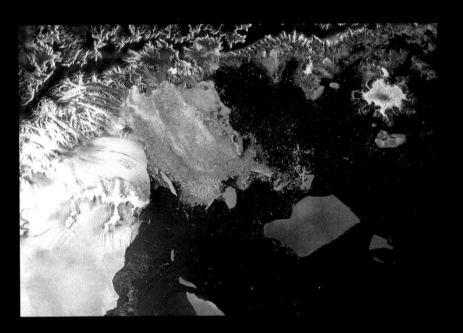

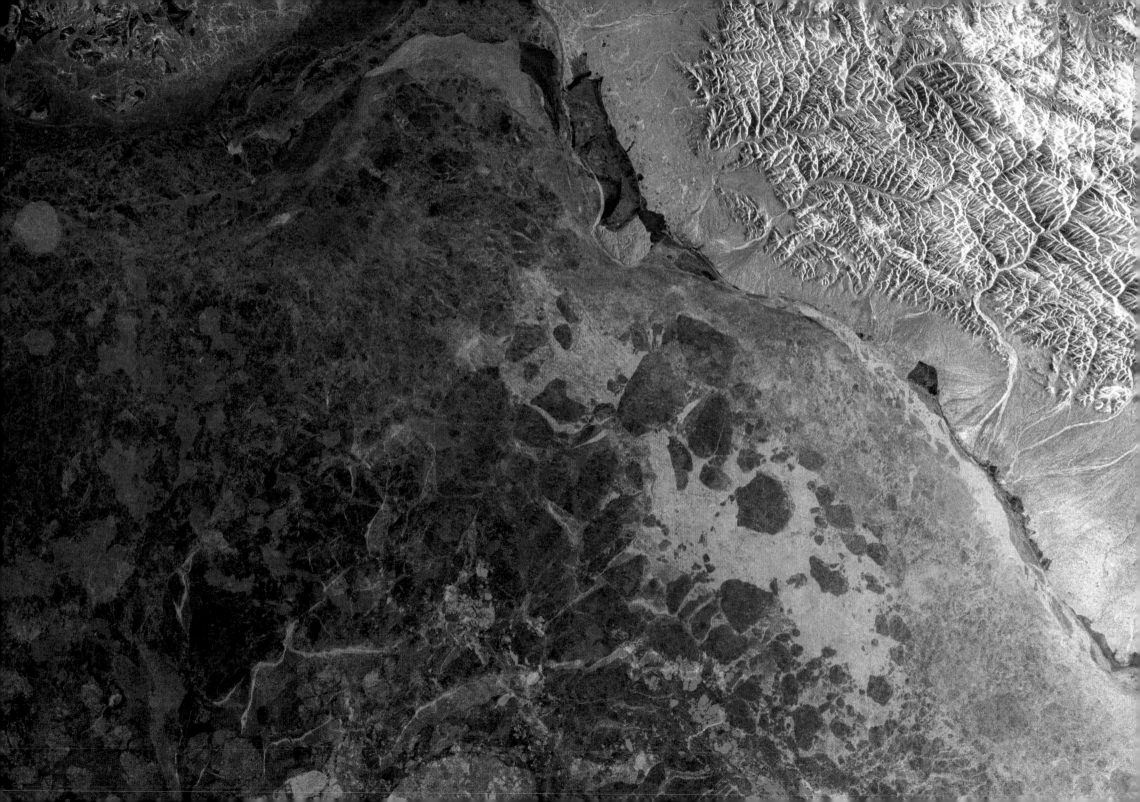

THE POLES BY NIGHT

The Earth's Poles by night (following pages) *recorded during the Arctic and Antarctic winter respectively. These composite images, processed by Germany's remote sensing data centre, are based on data obtained by the American NOAA 9 satellite in a large number of passes. The small black wedges represent zones where data could not be recorded by the satellite.*

Left: *the Beaufort Sea to the north of Alaska. The ice cover shown here was recorded by satellite over several months and then presented in different colours to indicate the different seasons.*

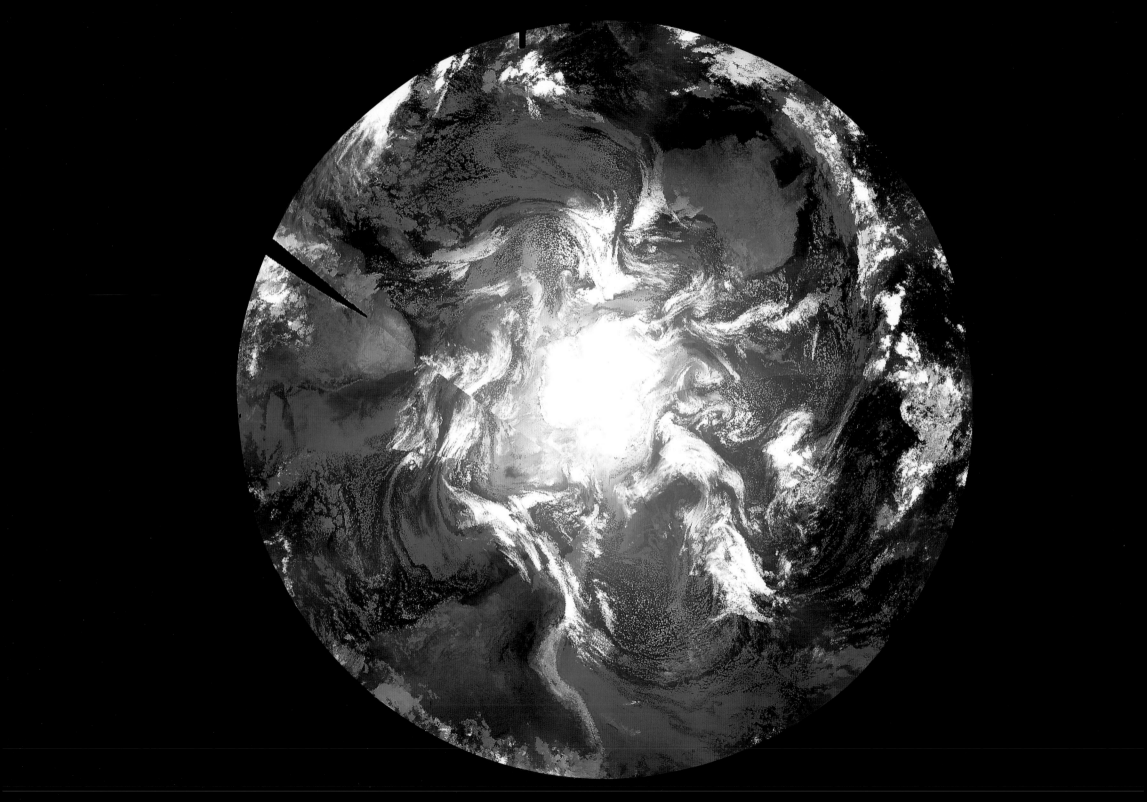

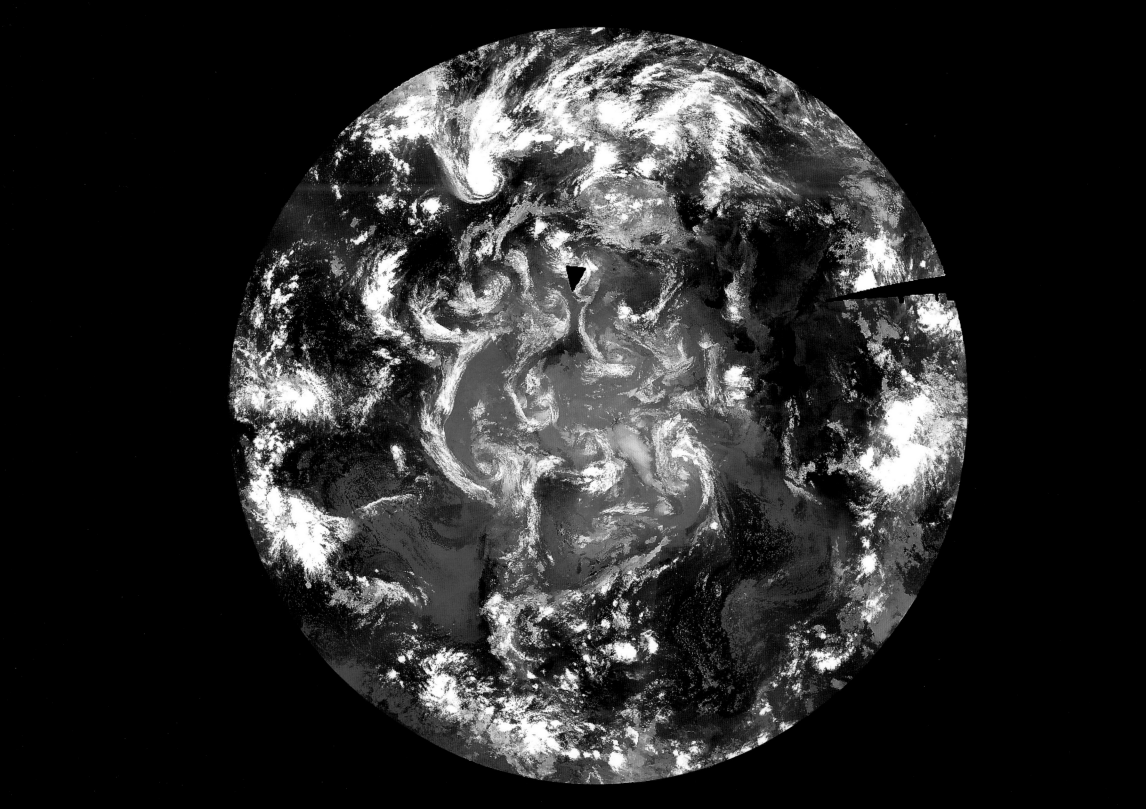

THE TOPSY-TURVY WORLD OF ZERO GRAVITY

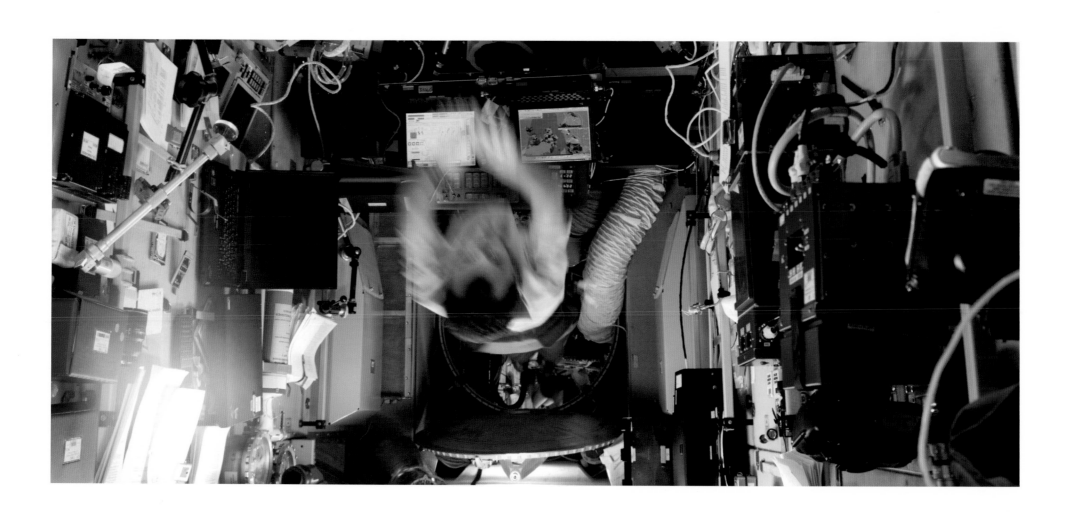

09

THE TOPSY-TURVY WORLD OF ZERO GRAVITY

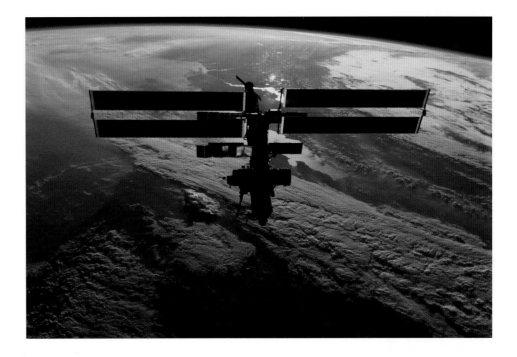

The International Space Station (ISS), right, represents the largest ever technology project based on international cooperation. Five partners from all around the world – the USA, Russia, European Space Agency (ESA) Member States, Canada and Japan – have joined forces to build this unique zero gravity research platform 400 kilometres above the Earth. Experiments that cannot possibly be carried out on the ground are resulting in important discoveries in areas as diverse as medicine or materials science, both in fundamental research and in industrial applications.

However, it is not merely in scientific terms that the Space Station can be considered a pioneering endeavour. It is also a symbol of peaceful cooperation, regardless of politics, and a piece of science fiction become reality – a kind of human "outpost" in space.

In the following pages, we accompany astronauts as they fly to the ISS, witness how they prepare for such missions, find out what a launch and zero gravity feel like and how they eventually get back to Earth.

Left: Spanish Astronaut Pedro Duque floating through the International Space Station (ISS).

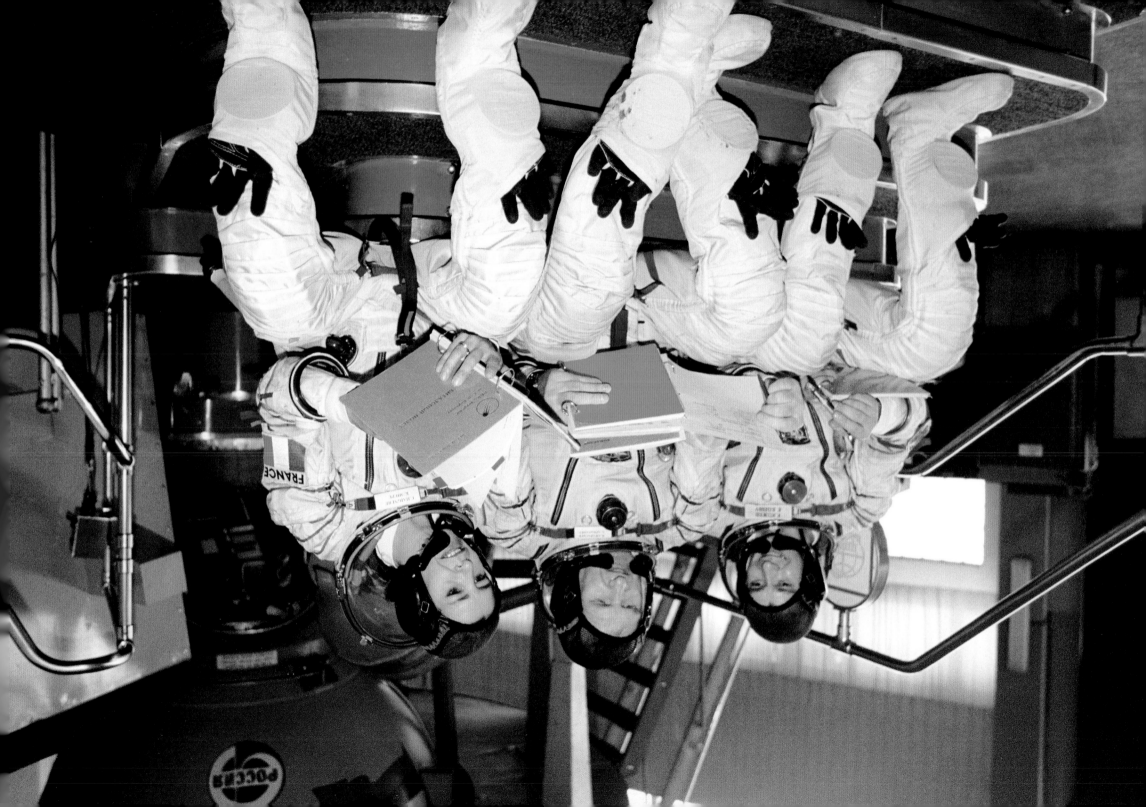

BACK TO THE CLASSROOM

Each space flight is preceded by an intensive programme of training, which begins in rather unglamorous fashion with long hours spent studying instructions and poring over manuals. Every last gesture is practised in simulators which are faithful reproductions of the spacecraft and Space Station modules astronauts will use.

Left: *French astronaut Claudie Haigneré (sitting, right) together with Russian colleagues at "Star City", as Moscow's Yuri Gagarin training centre is also known, before taking part in her second space mission. After carrying out numerous experiments on board Russia's Mir Space Station in 1996, she also flew to the International Space Station in October 2001.*

UNDERWATER PREPARATIONS FOR SPACE

Rehearsals take place in large diving pools for extra-vehicular activities (EVA) in which astronauts leave the ISS to work outside in space. The buoyancy experienced under water reproduces the near weightless conditions they will find in space. Astronauts soon discover that every movement requires much more time and effort when they do not have their feet firmly on the ground and have to work in the confines of a spacesuit.

Left: *underwater training for astronauts.*

Above right: *ESA astronaut Reinhold Ewald from Germany before taking part in a diving exercise.*
Below right: *parabolic flights, in which a purpose-built plane climbs steeply and then plummets earthwards in order to mimic a space-craft's trajectory, produce sequences of weightlessness lasting about 20 seconds. After each sequence, the pilot then regains control of the aircraft and brings it back on an upward course before beginning the next parabolic manoeuvre. Astronaut Roberto Vittori from Italy can be seen floating at the top of the picture near the middle.*

TRAINING FOR THE WORST CASE

Much of the training is spent preparing for emergencies. An astronaut has to keep a cool head even when things turn critical. German astronaut Reinhold Ewald, together with American and Russian colleagues, successfully dealt with one such critical situation when a serious fire broke out in 1997 on board the Mir Space Station. For a whole night the crew fought against the flames and smoke until, largely thanks to their excellent training, they were able to bring the problem under control.

Left: *Belgian astronaut Frank De Winne practises an emergency splash-down procedure in a Russian Soyuz capsule. In normal circumstances, the capsule's descent is slowed by parachute before touching down on dry land.*

Top right: *Roberto Vittori taking part in survival training. Astronauts also have to be able to cope with extreme cold should the rescue services be delayed after they return to Earth.*

Bottom right: *Italy's Umberto Guidoni learning how to evacuate the Space Shuttle in the event of a problem on landing. In April 2001, he became the first European to fly on board the ISS.*

COUNTDOWN TO LIFT-OFF

JUST THE TIP OF THE ICEBERG

In the course of their training, astronauts are not only taught how to operate instruments and react to emergencies. Another crucial component of their training relates to the experiments they must carry out in space. Astronauts visit the research institutes where the experiments are developed, familiarising themselves with the science involved and practising with ground models. When all the training exercises have been completed, the crew makes its way to the launch site – in the case of Russian Soyuz rockets, Baikonur in Kazakhstan or, for American missions, the Kennedy Space Center in Florida. Several days before launch, the astronauts have to go into quarantine to minimise the risk of falling ill at the last minute. This is because, in zero gravity, the effectiveness of the immune system is considerably reduced with the result that a simple case of the flu can become a serious problem. On launch day, it is only the astronauts' closest colleagues who are able to bid them farewell before they are taken to the launch pad in special buses. A few hours before lift-off, they take to their seats and begin checking the onboard systems, as they have done in training so many times before, until the countdown gets under way and the command is given to ignite the engines.

Left: *André Kuipers of the Netherlands shortly before a launch.*

It is not only the astronauts who are extremely busy preparing for a launch. On launch day, engineers and technicians activate all systems. In the control centres, the experts take up their positions and scientists prepare to assess the data. Thus, in a sense, astronauts are just the tip of the iceberg: part of a big team and a worldwide effort.

Following pages: *a Soyuz rocket is rolled out to the launch pad.*

With a deafening roar, the launch vehicle lifts off. The enormous thrust forces the astronauts inside back against their seats, subjecting them to pressure equal to many times their body weight. However, after about eight minutes, when orbit is reached and the engines are shut down, zero gravity abruptly takes hold: after being exposed to powerful acceleration that leaves the pulse racing and shaken by the shuddering and vibration of the powerful engines, the astronauts suddenly find themselves plunged into another world. Everything that is not strapped down or attached in some other way begins floating around the spacecraft. The noise of the engines is replaced by the stillness of space while from a height of several hundred kilometres the Earth is revealed in all its majesty. However there is not much time to enjoy the

CRITICAL MANOEUVRES HIGH ABOVE THE EARTH

After two days, the Soyuz capsule is in sight of the Space Station. Both are now circling the Earth at a speed of 28,000 kilometres per hour. The Soyuz with its three-cosmonaut crew is able to dock with the ISS automatically. However, if the commander is required to intervene, he switches to manual operation and guides the spacecraft towards the docking assembly. Once checks have been carried out on all systems, the air locks are opened and the new crew float through into the Station. The docking procedures are similar for the Space Shuttle, the main difference being that it can carry more astronauts and larger payloads.

Having handed the Station over to the new arrivals, the old crew returns to Earth within a few days. The new shift, however, must now spend half a year in orbit. During the construction phase the Station will at times be crewed by only two astronauts – later that number should rise to as much as seven. The remaining berths in Soyuz and the Space Shuttle are therefore reserved for astronauts on short mis-sions to conduct experiments. In such cases, they fly to the ISS with the replacement crew and come back down with the old one.

Left: *a Soyuz capsule docking, photographed through one of the Space Station windows.* Above right: *a Space Shuttle closing in.*

Below right: *Roberto Vittori entering the Space Station.*

16 SUNRISES IN A SINGLE DAY

Weightlessness takes a certain amount of getting used to. Many gestures which are routine on Earth have to be rethought. Astronauts have to strap themselves in to go to sleep, otherwise they end up floating around the cabin. They use wet towels instead of showers, which are impracticable because the water droplets would float around inside the spacecraft. Even the sense of taste is affected, something for which no explanation had been found until recently. The fact that there is no "up" or "down" can give rise to feelings of disorientation. And since it takes 90 minutes to orbit the Earth, it is possible to witness 16 sunrises and 16 sunsets each day, something which can quite easily interfere with people's "inner clocks".

Left: *Claudie Haigneré, the first woman from Europe to visit the Space Station.*

Right: *time permitting, simple experiments can be carried out on camera, which can, in a fun way, get schoolchildren interested in science and research.*

Following pages: *the Earth seen from space.*

KEEPING THE CREW SUPPLIED

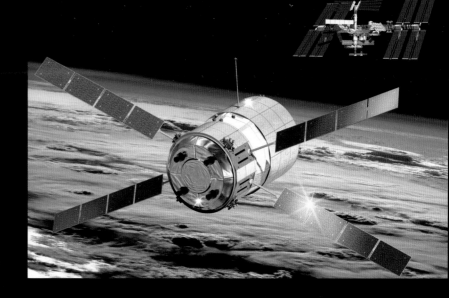

Power generation using high-efficiency solar cells, multiple redundant onboard computer systems, automatic trajectory correction – due to the extreme conditions in space, the construction and operation of a Space Station presents particular technical challenges. As a result, the on-board systems of the ISS are among the finest examples of the engineer's art. For example, since the crew needs more water than can be transported to the Station, condensation from their breathing is filtered and reprocessed into drinking water. Nonetheless, the crew must receive regular supplies of food, spare parts and experimental equipment. To date, this task has principally been performed by Russian Progress cargo ships, although their carrying capacity is limited. In the future, the plan is to use Europe's Automatic Transfer Vehicle (ATV) to transport loads of up to nine tonnes to the ISS.

Along with the ATV and the ERA robotic arm, Europe's most important contribution to the ISS is the Columbus module. This flying laboratory will dock with the ISS and allow high quality research to be carried out in zero gravity conditions.

Left: *the Progress capsule.*

Above right: *artist's impression of the ATV. Below: an ATV being assembled at the Alenia Spazio facility in Turin, Italy.*

Following pages: *preparation of the Columbus laboratory at EADS in Bremen, Germany (Image: EADS, Kurt Henseler).*

A FIRST-RATE PLATFORM FOR RESEARCH

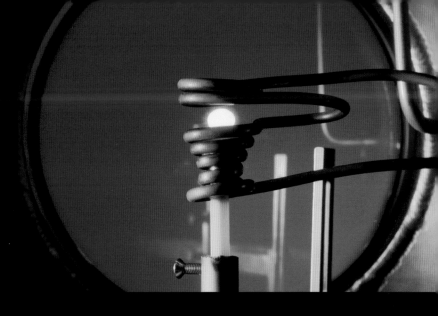

In weightless conditions, it is possible to study many effects that cannot be studied on the ground due to the effects of gravity. Experiments frequently bring results of significance to a great many activities beyond space. Besides disciplines such as materials sciences or biology, human medicine is also an important field of research. This is because in zero gravity the human organism develops symptoms of all sorts of illnesses: for example, bones lose calcium as in cases of osteoporosis, the cardiocirculatory system changes, the sense of balance is impaired and the immune system deteriorates rapidly. A few days after returning to Earth, the symptoms subside completely. Therefore, scientists are able to investigate both the onset of an illness and the subsequent return to health under precisely controlled laboratory conditions. In many cases, the discoveries made in this way have long since been incorporated into established medical practice.

Left: *in weightless conditions, it is possible to study more closely certain processes involved in the heating and solidification of metallic melts, which on Earth are "obscured" by the omnipresent gravitational force. Knowledge gained in this way can subsequently be used to optimise manufacturing processes.*

Above right: *experiments in materials science. Below: an unusual portrait of a NASA astronaut, taken through a drop of water suspended in mid-air due to weightlessness.*

STEPPING OUT ... INTO SPACE

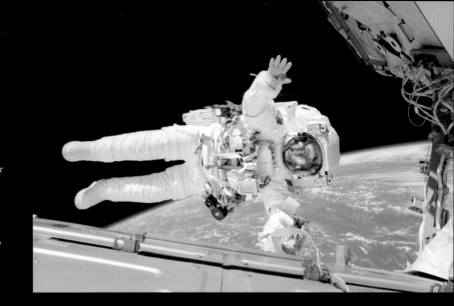

Contrary to what the term might suggest, "space walks" place some of the most severe strain on the body to which an astronaut can be subjected. It is for that reason that during such activities, which often last several hours, data on all the important vital functions such as pulse and body temperature are relayed to ground control in real time for monitoring by doctors.

This technique of direct transmission of medical data has also been used in "telemedicine" on Earth. Thus, for example, doctors are able to remotely monitor the medical condition of small children threatened with Sudden Infant Death Syndrome. Parents can be alerted in an emergency and medical assistance called out. That way the baby is just as safe at home as it would be in hospital.

Left: *French astronaut Philippe Perrin performing a space walk. In 2002 he flew to the ISS on behalf of the French Space Agency, CNES.* Above right: *NASA astronaut Rex Walheim.*

Below right: *an at-risk baby with remote diagnosis sensors in its clothing. Similar sensors are to be found in astronauts' undergarments.*

IMPRESSIONS FROM ORBIT

The Space Shuttle pictured in front of an Earth bathed in sunlight.

Following pages, left: *the International Space Station (ISS).*
Following pages, right: *a NASA astronaut pictured on a space walk with the Earth and Sun in the background.*

After the launch itself, re-entry into the Earth's atmosphere and landing are among the most critical phases in a mission. In simple terms, after undocking, Space Shuttles or Soyuz capsules reduce speed, and thus automatically drop to lower orbits and draw closer to the Earth. In addition, they are subject to an increasingly strong braking effect from the lower, denser atmospheric layers. Whereas the Shuttle carries out a series of complicated flight manoeuvres, the Russian capsule descends towards the Earth on a predetermined trajectory. Finally, its flight is slowed one last time by parachutes and by the ignition of a braking engine. The Space Shuttle, for its part, lands like an aeroplane.

eft: a Soyuz capsule floats towards the ground supported by a para-

SIGHTS AND INSIGHTS: HOW ASTRONAUTS VIEW THE EARTH

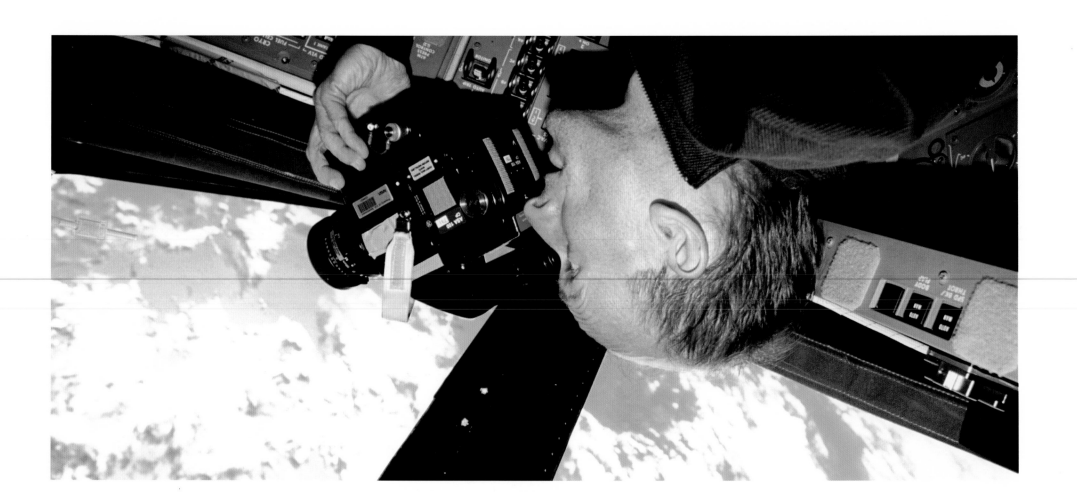

SIGHTS AND INSIGHTS:
HOW ASTRONAUTS VIEW THE EARTH

When astronauts journey into space, they do so in the interests of science. However, in addition to the many experimental results and discoveries astronauts bring back to Earth, they also return with insights of a quite different kind. Their accounts often centre around the same themes: the uniqueness of our planet, its incredible beauty and manifest vulnerability. Subsequently, when recounting their experiences at the many events they attend, their core message is often that we must treat the Earth and its natural resources with great care for the good of our children and future generations.

The following pages contain some of the most beautiful images of our "blue planet" as seen through the eyes of astronauts in orbit around it.

Left: ESA astronaut Gerhard Thiele from Germany looks out in wonder from the window of the Space Shuttle. When his on-board schedule permits, Thiele records his impressions on film. Right: the Earth pictured from orbit.

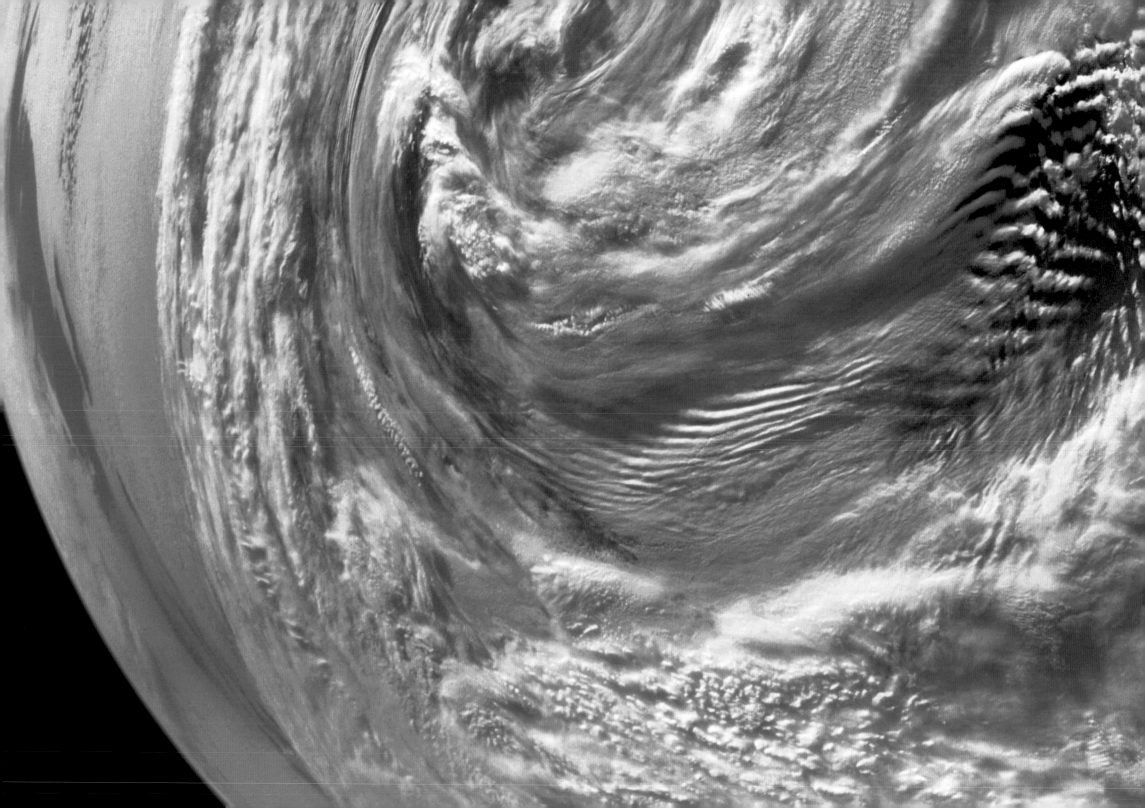

OUR PLANET FROM 400 KILOMETRES UP

Left: *a cyclone seen from space.*

Above right: *the world's second highest peak, the legendary K2. From 400 kilometres up, even this giant among mountains appears tiny.*
Below right: *Iran's Zagros mountains on the Persian Gulf coast.*

Following pages, left: *evening over the Indian Ocean.*
Following pages, right: *view from one of the windows of the International Space Station.*

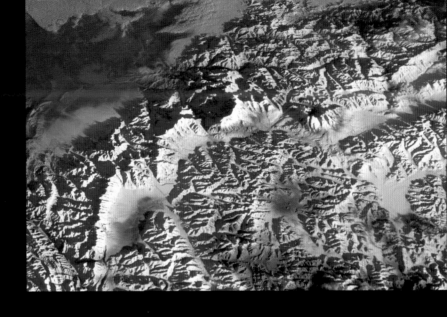

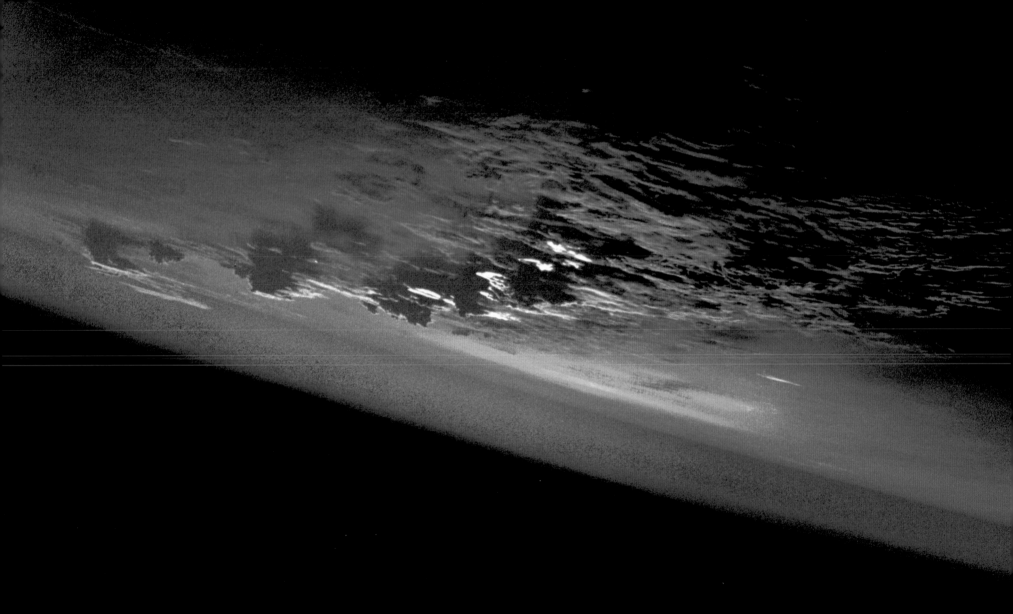

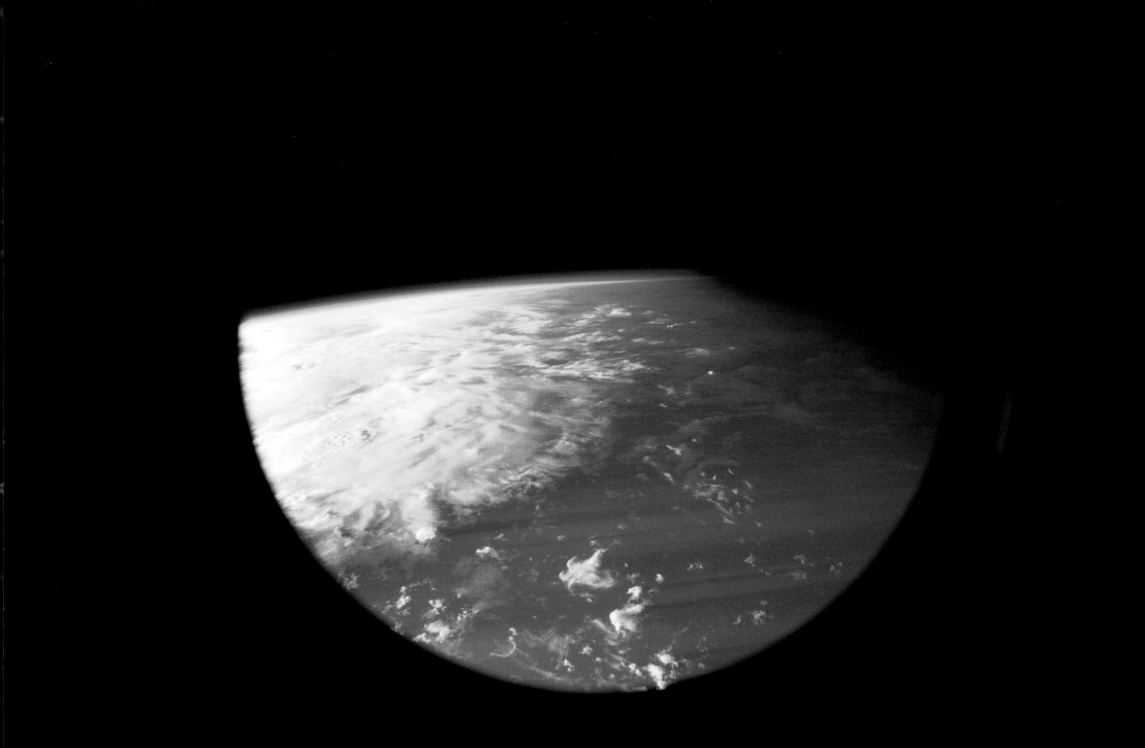

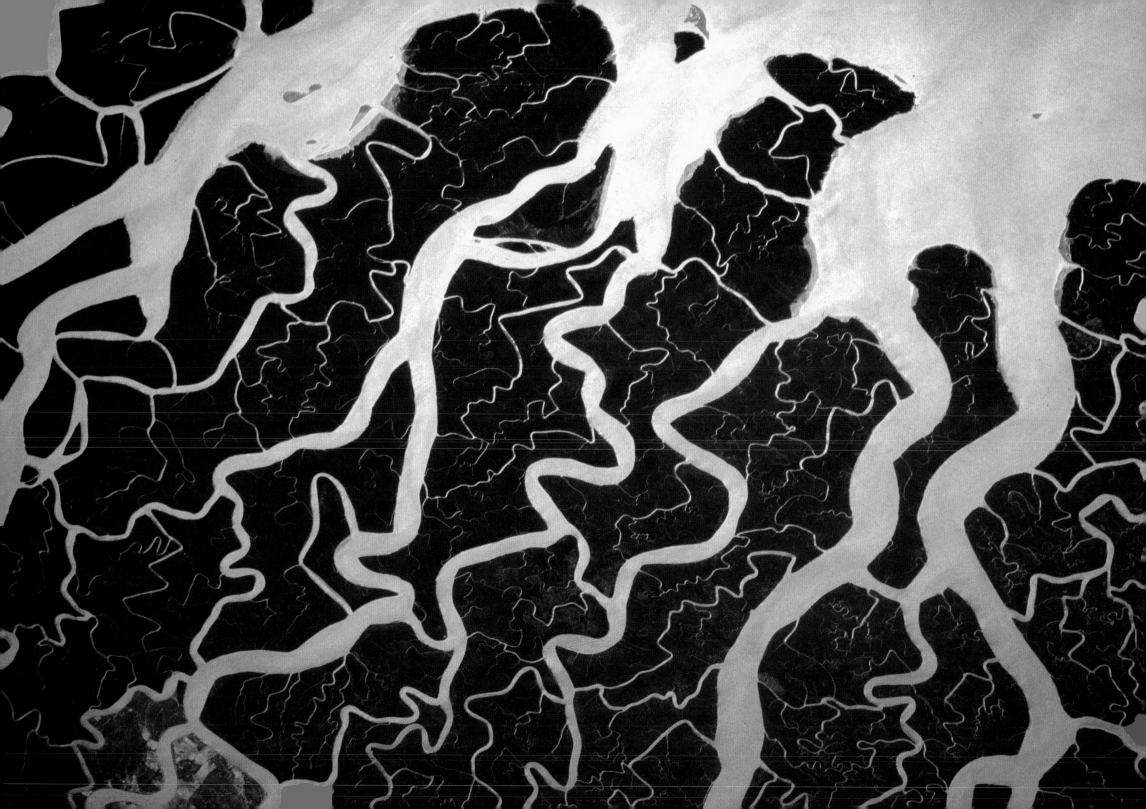

THE WORLD'S BIGGEST RIVER DELTA

Left: *the convergence of the Ganges and Brahmaputra rivers gives rise to the biggest river delta in the world. While the Ganges emerges to the south of the Himalayas from the confluence of other rivers, starting in the north, the Brahmaputra flows around the Earth's most gigantic mountain range in an enormous loop.*

Following pages, left: *Mount Everest.*
Following pages, right: *the horizon as seen from space. The pink layer is the result of sulphur emissions from a volcanic eruption in the Philippines.*

10

CROSSING CONTINENTS IN MINUTES

Travelling at a speed of 28,000 kilometres per hour, astronauts fly over continents and oceans in a matter of minutes.

Left: *the Kamchatka peninsula in Russia's far east is one of the most volcanically active regions on Earth.*

Right: *the Chinese city of Shenyang in winter.*

Double page spread, overleaf: *the Scott and Seringapatam Reefs off northwestern Australia.*

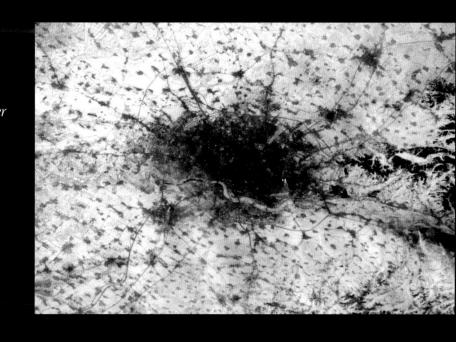

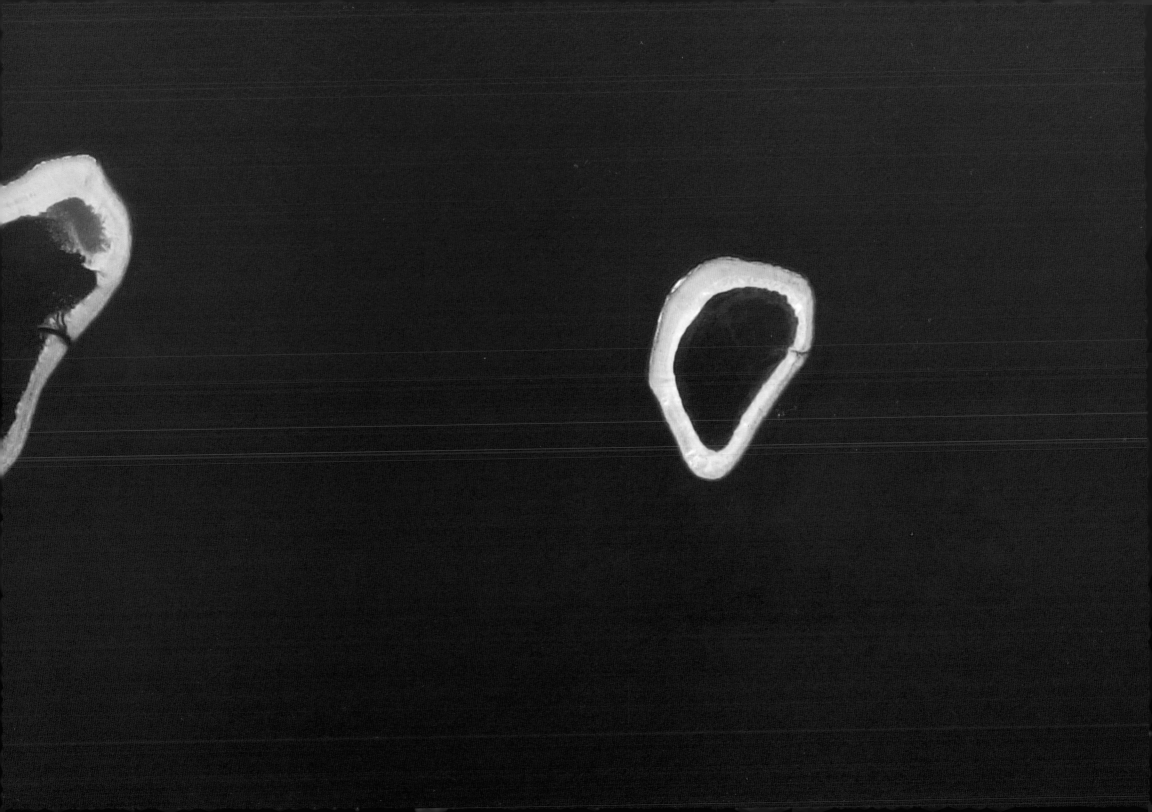

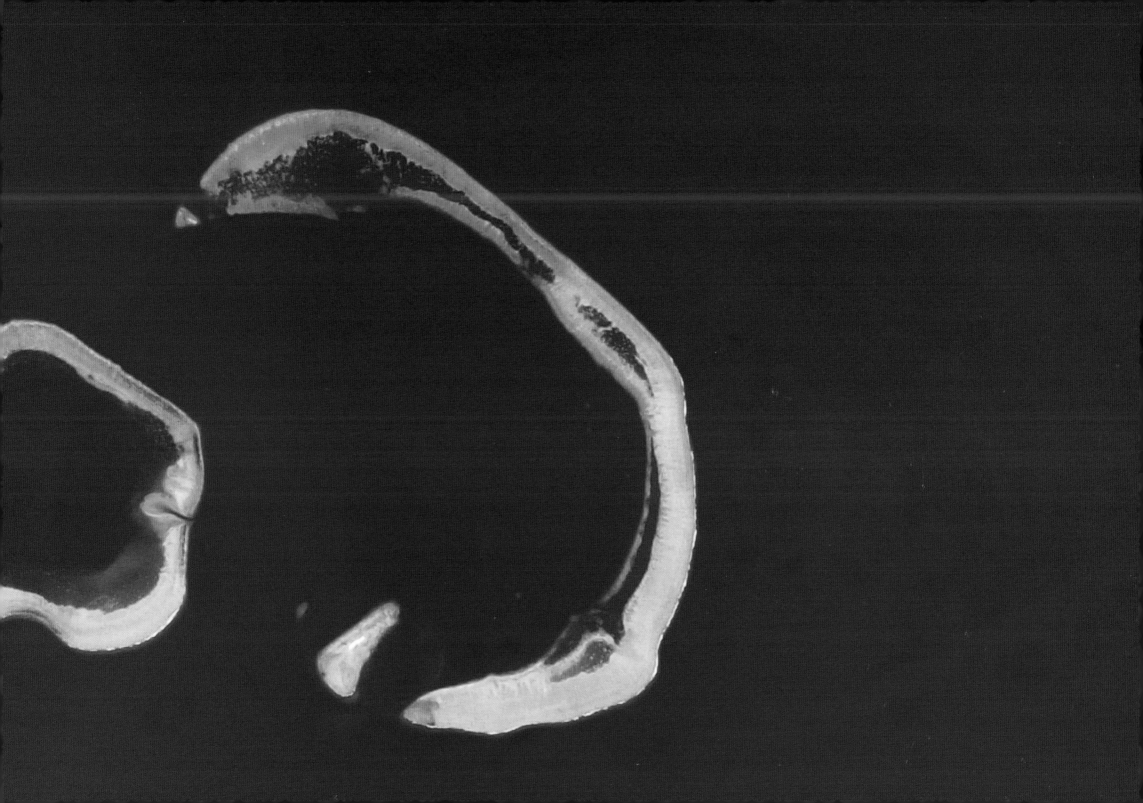

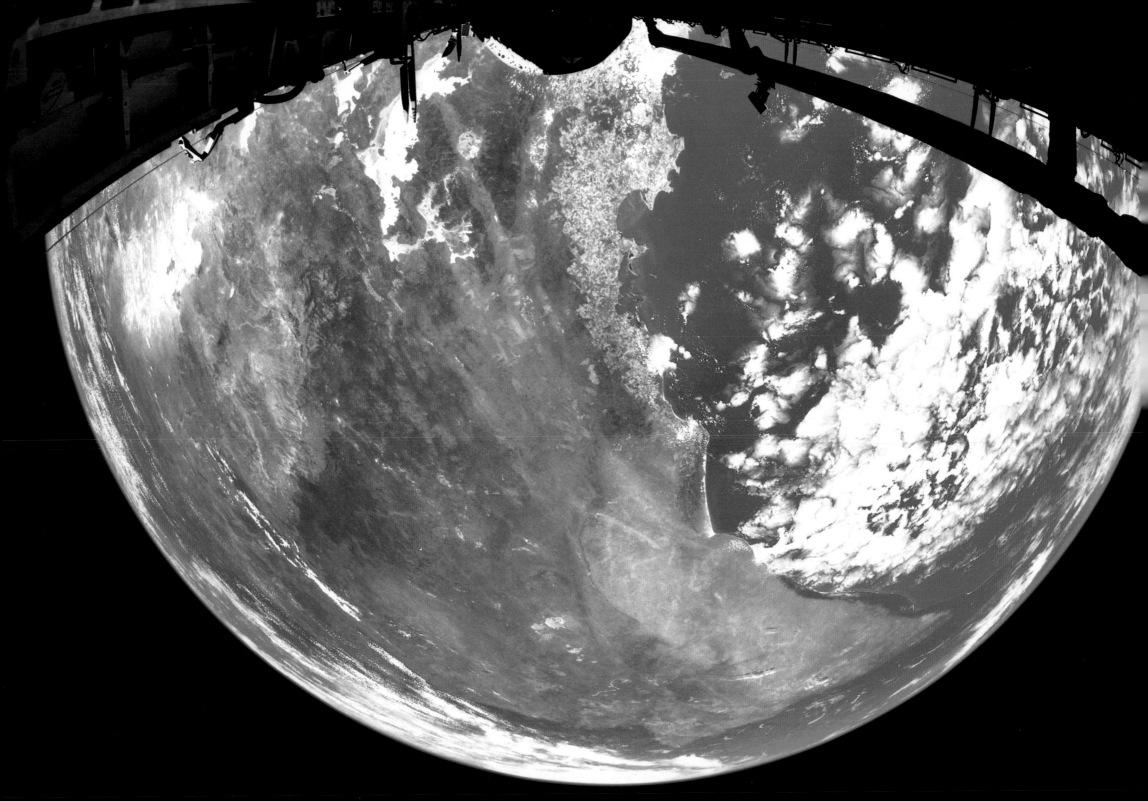

Main picture, left: *the Earth with Australia looming large, as seen from the Shuttle flight deck aft windows. In the foreground is the empty cargo bay of the Shuttle Endeavour. It had previously contained an American element of the International Space Station, which was subsequently joined to Russia's Zarya module. The photograph was taken with an IMAX large-format camera.*

Right: *the De Grey River estuary in Western Australia. It does not take a great deal of imagination to make out the form of a fish or mythical creature in the contours of the landscape – not that astronauts have that much time for such musings.*

SEEING AND BEING SEEN

In this photograph of New York, it is even possible to distinguish individual streets. In the centre of the picture is Manhattan, flanked by the Hudson and East Rivers. Right: *Miami Beach.*

It is also possible to spot the Space Station from the ground, albeit only in the early morning or late evening: only at dawn and dusk does it stand out against the dark night sky, illuminated by oblique rays from the Sun, before disappearing below the horizon again within the space of a few minutes.

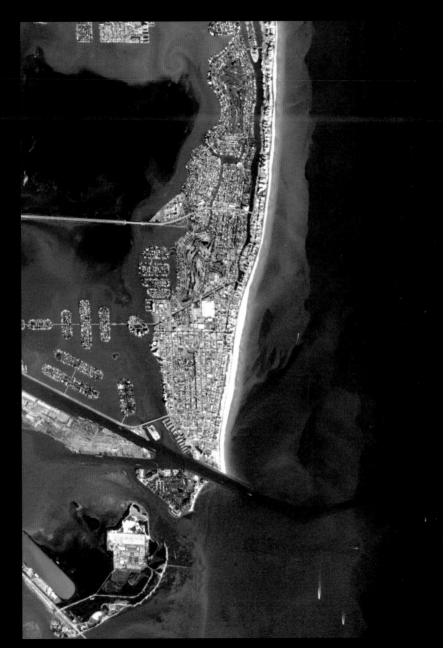

SURVEYING LANDSCAPES FROM SPACE

Left: *the heightened perspective obtained from space means that it is possible to perceive a landscape's relief as in this picture of the Colorado River in the United States of America.*

Following pages, left: *an infrared image of southern California (to the top of the picture) on the border with Mexico (below) showing the differing land use in the two areas.*
Following pages, right: *the icy mountainous landscape of Alaska.*

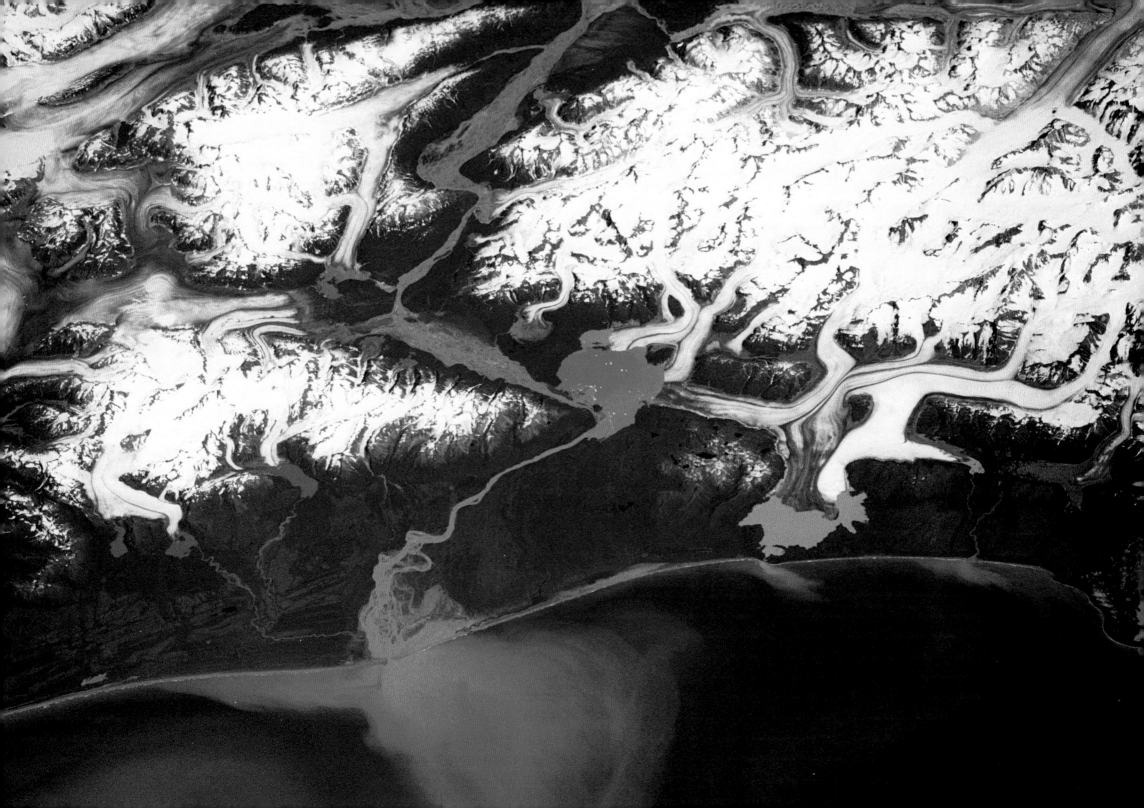

ISLANDS, ICE AND METEOR CRATERS

All three images on these pages are of Canada:

Left: *an icebound St James Bay.*

Above right: *Nova Scotia, Prince Edward Island and Cape Breton Island.*

Below right: *the Manicouagan impact crater, Quebec Province, eastern Canada. This unusual formation was caused by a meteorite impact some 200 million years ago.*

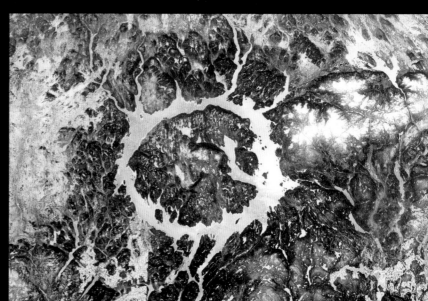

EARTH, THE WATER PLANET

Left: *the Atlantic bathed in sunlight. Most of the regions astronauts fly over are not landmass but instead are covered by the Earth's gigantic oceans.*

The right-hand picture shows the Shuttle's robotic arm, which can be operated from the flight deck.

123

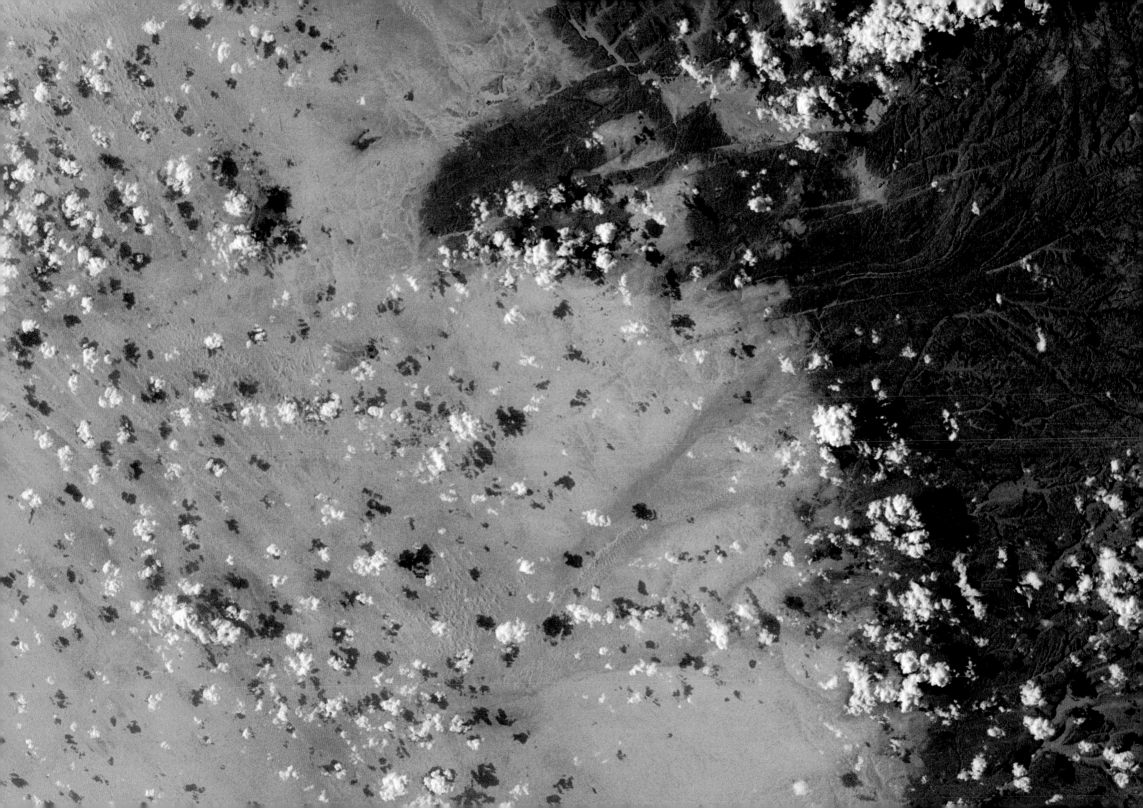

CIRCLES IN THE DESERT

The strange circular structures in Saudi Arabia, below right, are in fact artificially irrigated fields in which groundwater is extracted from a depth of several hundred metres. The circular shape is due to the fact that irrigation is carried out in a concentric circle around the borehole. Top right: *view over Algeria.*

Left: *clouds over the Sahara.*

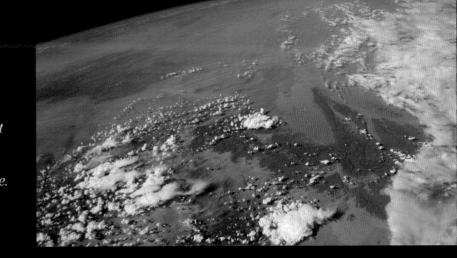

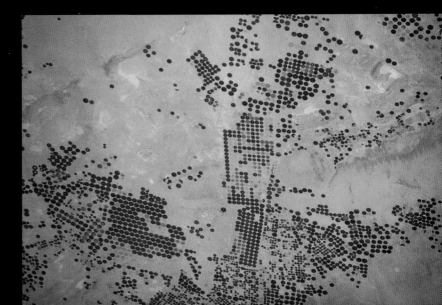

TRACES IN THE SAND

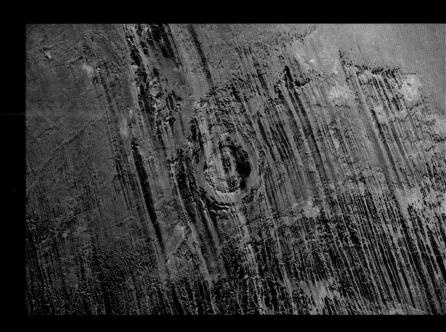

The Aorounga crater in Chad, above right, is a remarkable example of the traces left by a meteorite impact. In addition, the landscape is heavily marked by erosion, with the wind over millions of years having etched out grooved patterns, while at the same time partially filling the crater basin with sand.

Left: *sunset over the Sahara.*

Below right: *the Sinai Peninsula.*

Following pages: *a landscape of dunes in Africa (left) and a view over the north of the continent (right).*

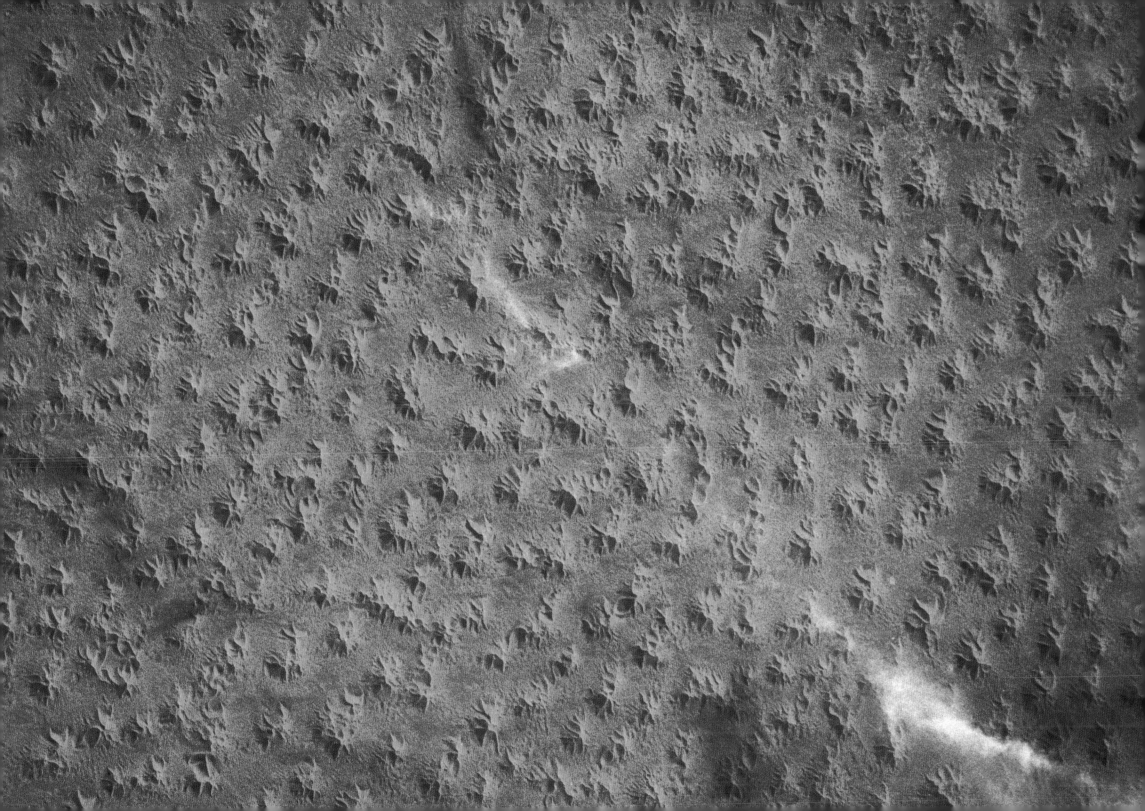

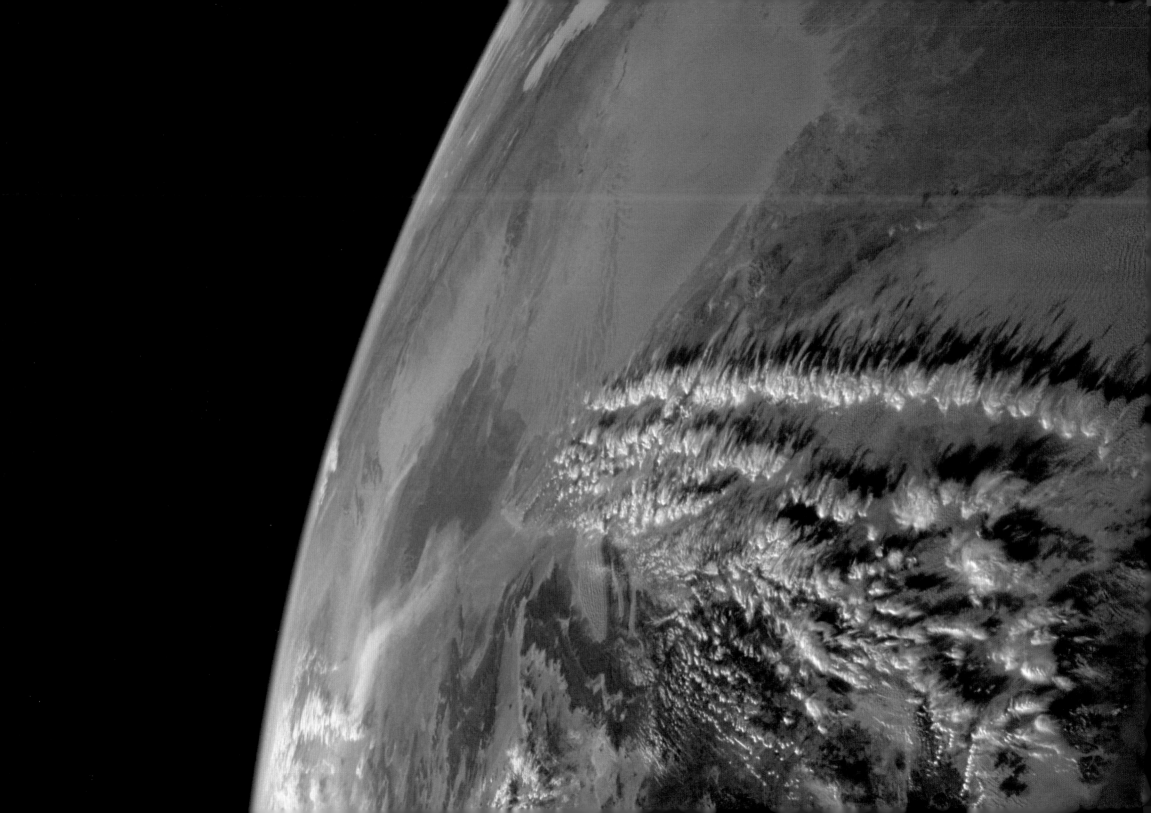

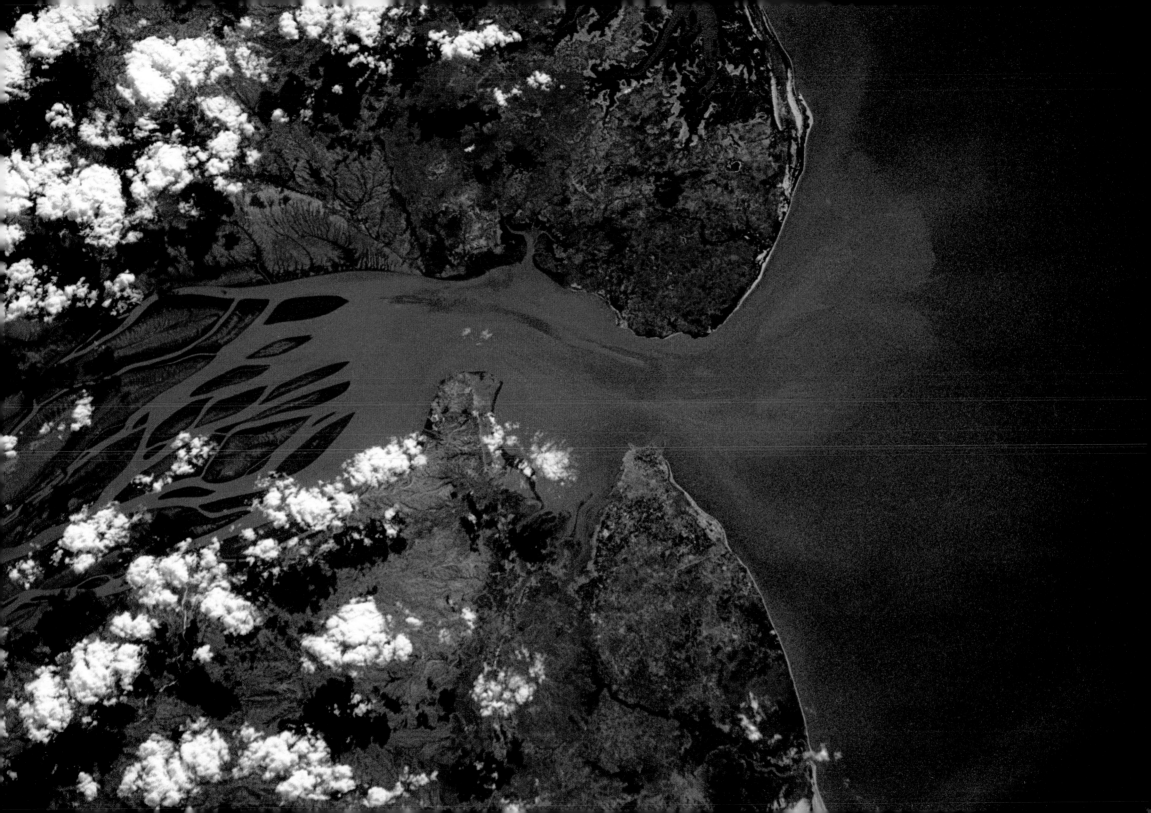

RED RIVERS ON THE BLUE PLANET

The reddish hue of Madagascar's largest river, the Betsiboka, (left) is due to the silt and other sediments released by logging. In the picture on the right, on the other hand, it is simply the oblique angle of the Sun which is responsible for bathing the coast of this east African island in a reddish evening light.

ISLANDS IN THE SUN

Left: *the Canary Islands bathed in sunlight reflected off the Atlantic.*

Right: *the Strait of Gibraltar, which forms the meeting point between two continents, with Europe (below) and Africa (above), and between two seas, with the Mediterranean (left) and the Atlantic (right).*

INFRARED BORDEAUX

Left: *Bordeaux in southwest France, in colours that bring to mind the region's famous wines. In this infrared image, it is possible to distinguish fields (in bright red) from woodland (in dark red). Clearly visible is the confluence of the Garonne and Dordogne rivers, which merge at this point to form the Gironde.*

Right: *the Swiss Alps with the Eiger, Jungfrau and Mönch mountains.*

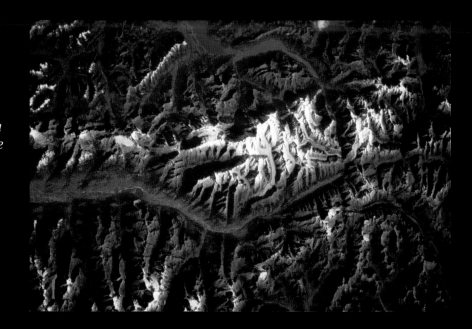

FLYING OVER A ROTATING GLOBE

The Mediterranean island of Crete (left) and the tip of the Italian boot with Sicily in the background (right). Not all regions of the Earth are visible to the astronauts: the imaginary circle described by the ISS as it orbits the Earth is inclined by 51.6 degrees at the Equator. Consequently, at its northernmost and southernmost point, its orbit never extends beyond 52 degrees latitude, which in the north corresponds approximately to the level of Berlin and stretches to near Cape Horn in the southern hemisphere. Thus, each time the ISS circles the Earth, the globe rotates a little further, with the result that 90 minutes later the crew does not fly over the same region again, but instead flies over an area located further to the west.

FLITTING FROM DARKNESS TO LIGHT

Left: *clouds at dawn over Poland. Because the Space Shuttle and ISS only take 90 minutes to complete an orbit and that, consequently, they circle the Earth 16 times in 24 hours, astronauts frequently fly over the boundary between day and night.*

Double-page spread, overleaf: *cloud formations.*

139

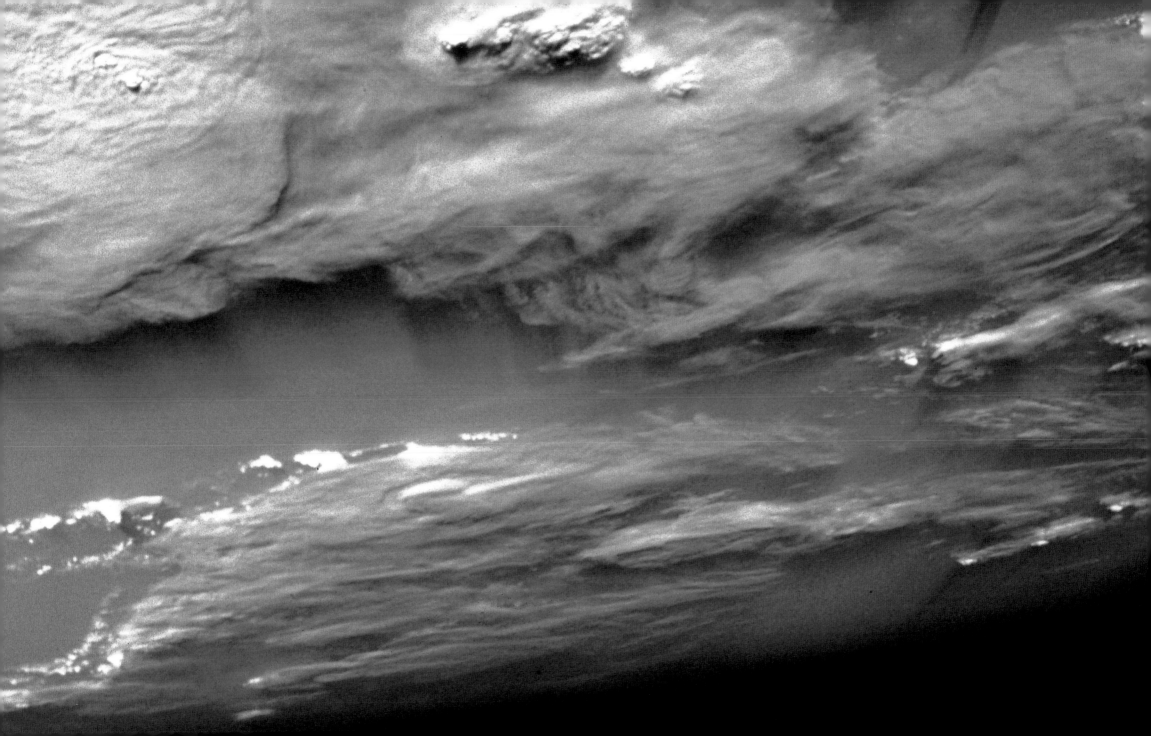

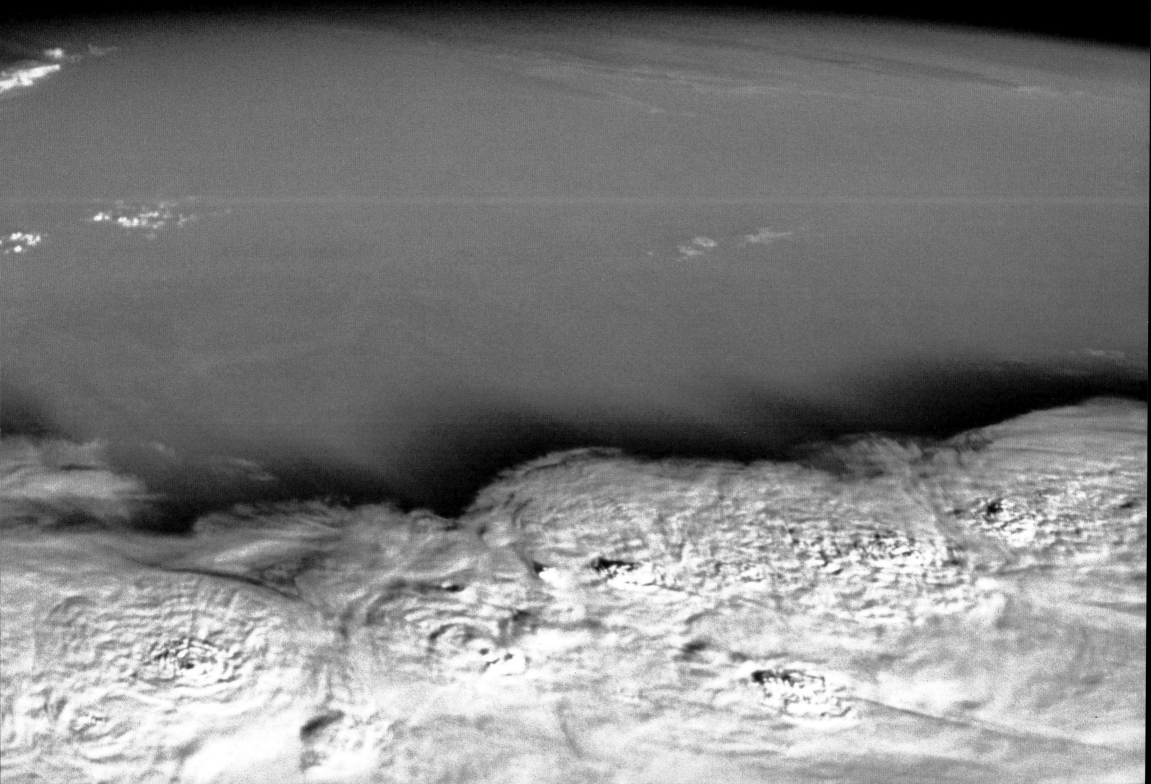

DROPPING IN ON OUR COSMIC NEIGHBOURS

DROPPING IN ON OUR COSMIC NEIGHBOURS

Nine planets revolve around the Sun – some, like Mercury and Venus, at close quarters and others at a distance of many hundred million kilometres, from which point even our mighty Sun looks like nothing more than a bright star. As the third innermost planet, the Earth is at the ideal distance from the Sun; this, among many other factors, is what makes it possible for life to flourish on our planet at all. However, other celestial bodies could also harbour simple life forms. After all, we know of bacteria which exist on Earth even under extreme conditions such as in freezing polar ice or close to seabed "hotspots" where no sunlight ever penetrates. Thus, the search for signs of past or even presently existing life is not some mere flight of fancy, but is one of the main forces driving the exploration of our Solar System.

Yet, however far these missions to distant worlds may take us, they also help us gain a better understanding of the history of our own planet's development. One of many such examples is ESA's Rosetta mission, the aim of which is to land an unmanned probe on a comet.

Comets generally describe their trajectories far beyond the outer planets, many millions or even billions of kilometres from us, and form their characteristic tail when, as happens from time to time, they move into the vicinity of the Sun. In these cold celestial bodies, the matter from which they and the whole Solar System, including the Earth, was formed some five billion years ago is preserved as if in a cosmic "deep freeze". Therefore, by analysing the composition of a comet, we are also looking back into the past to examine the early stages of the Earth's formation.

In the following pages, you will be invited on a journey of discovery through the Solar System, witnessing some of the most fascinating space missions of our time, beginning with the Sun itself and continuing on out towards Saturn's mysterious moon, Titan, and the little-explored outer planets.

Left: artist's impression of the European Huygens probe landing on Saturn's moon, Titan. The Solar System's second biggest moon is the only one with a dense atmosphere. Scientists believe that it resembles the atmosphere of the infant Earth and that it will therefore further their understanding of the early history of our own planet.

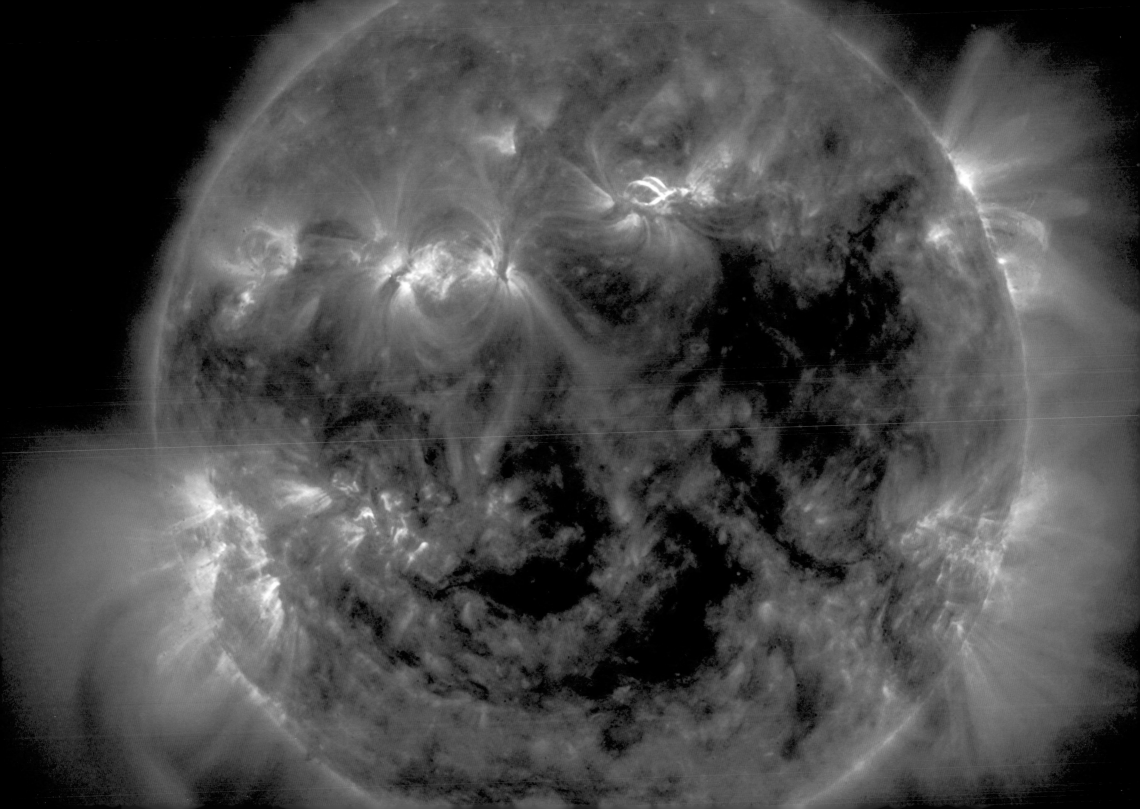

WHEN THE SUN SHINES BLUE

SPECTACULAR CLOSE-UPS

Solar research enables us to study our central star and the effects of the Sun's rays on life on Earth. To that end, for example, studies are carried out into the effects on the Earth's magnetosphere of solar wind (a stream of particles which can at times grow dangerously in intensity). If this protective shield around our planet is not able to cope with such an increased particle bombardment, the effects could even include temporary disruption of the functioning of power stations.

Science also benefits from solar probes: after all, the Sun, at "only" 150 million kilometres from the Earth, is the nearest star, which can thus be studied from close range. Of all solar probes, the most remarkable is without doubt SOHO, a project carried out in close cooperation between Europe and the United States. SOHO studies the processes taking place in the Sun's interior, on its surface and in its turbulent atmosphere, from which vast quantities of solar matter are hurled into space. Incidentally, these "protuberances", as they are called, are many times the size of the Earth. The "blue Sun" (left) is the result of a SOHO instrument recording in a particular segment of the ultraviolet light spectrum, which provides indications as to temperature distribution.

Below: *a spectacular image from NASA's Trace probe showing just how turbulent conditions are on the Sun.*

Following pages: *another picture from the SOHO solar probe showing a massive eruption, or protuberance.*

147

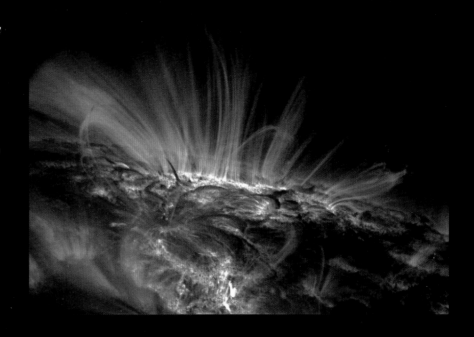

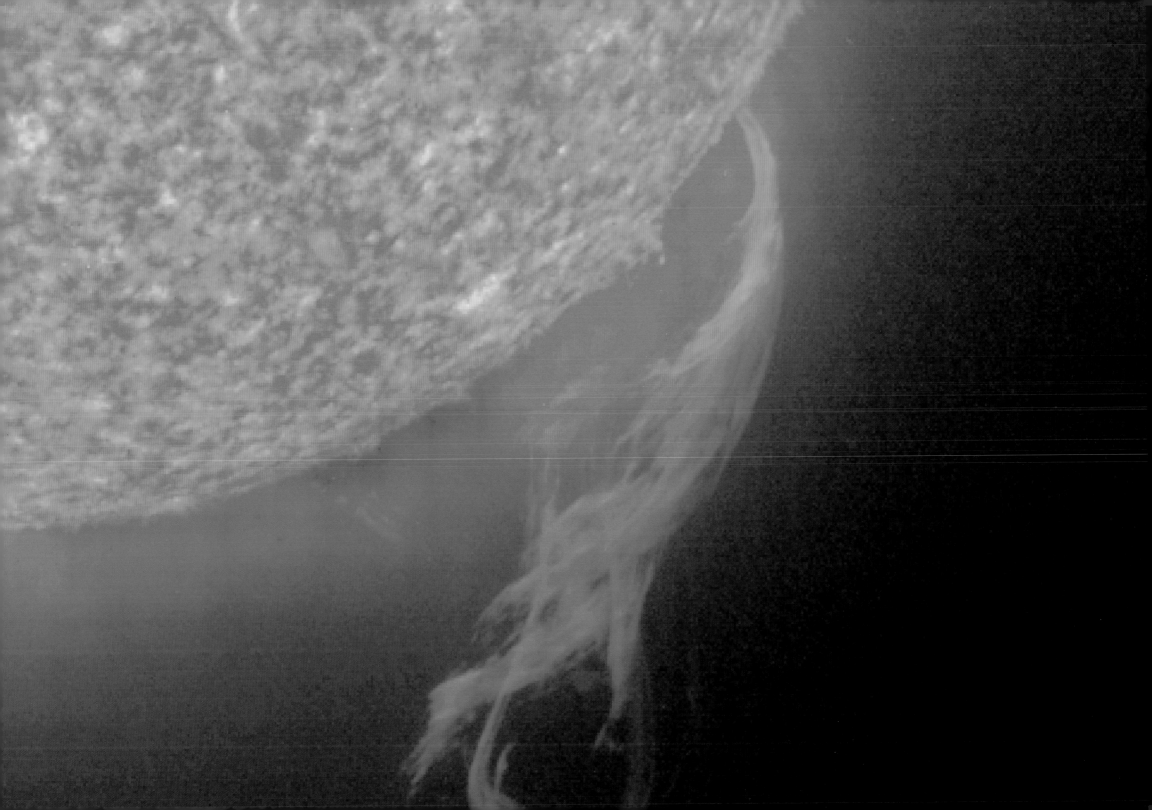

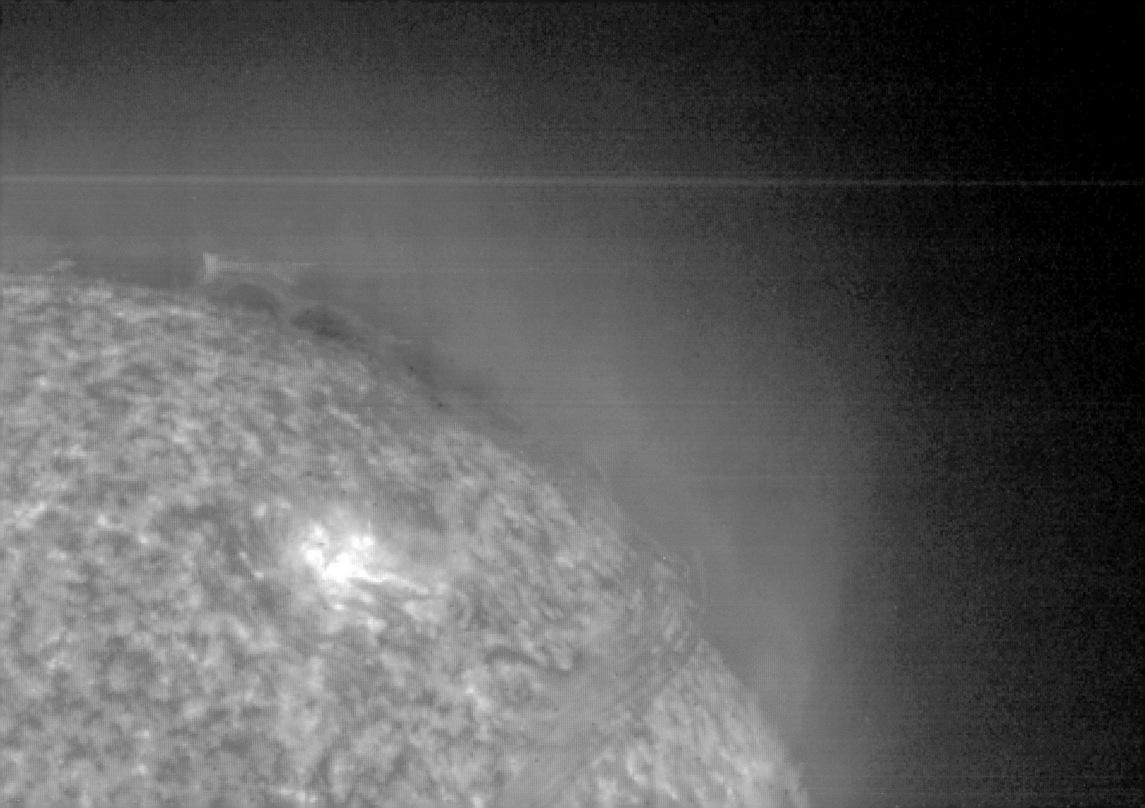

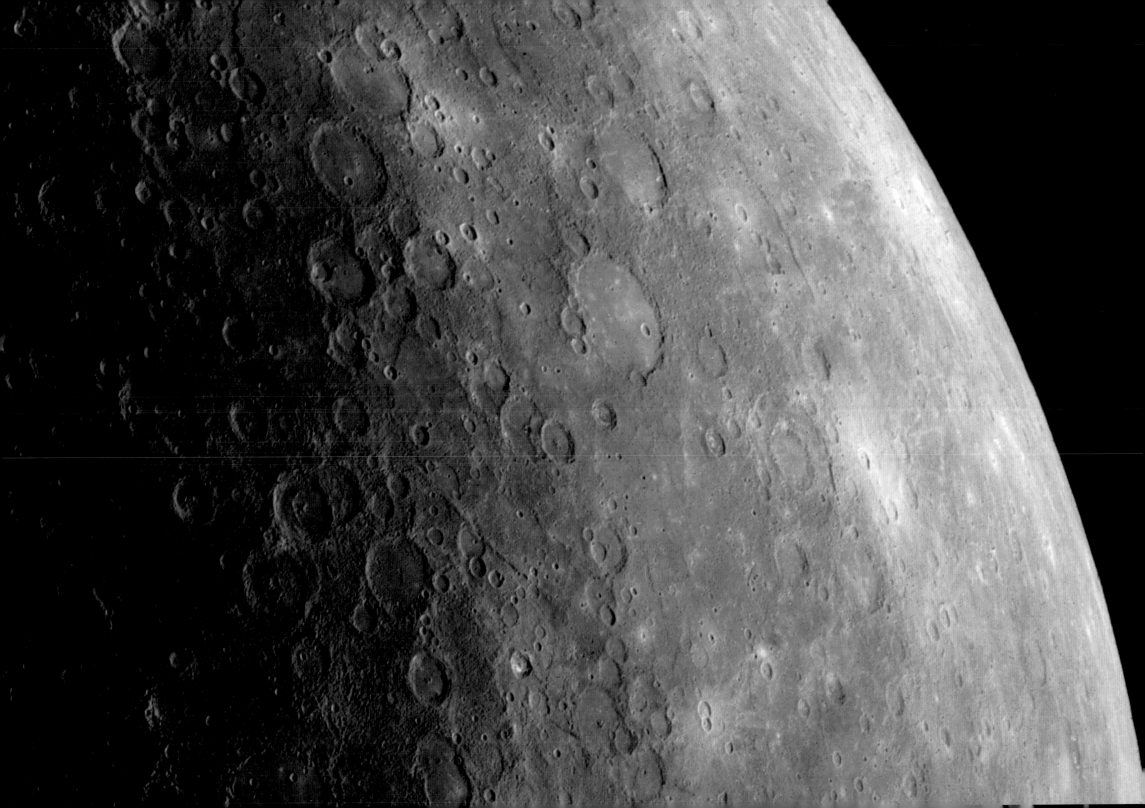

Mercury is the least explored of the inner Solar System planets. Some parts of its surface still remain to be photographed and are thus shown as blank areas on the map. The United States and Europe currently intend to send probes to Mercury to find answers to a whole range of questions. For example, was there once a catastrophe of unimaginable proportions in which a massive celestial body collided with Mercury? There is definitely a certain amount of evidence for such an impact, which could have occurred billions of years ago. This might explain why Mercury's geological composition is different from that of its fellow inner planets, Venus, Earth and Mars. And is it possible likewise to draw conclusions from this impact theory concerning the origins of our Moon, which might have been created in an equally dramatic collision between the Earth and another celestial body? Mercury would appear to have some interesting tales to tell researchers. However, to fly there would mean overcoming a number of challenges. For instance, probes would have to be able to withstand extreme temperatures if they were to orbit a planet that close to the Sun. To go there would mean setting off on a blisteringly hot journey to the centre of our Solar System.

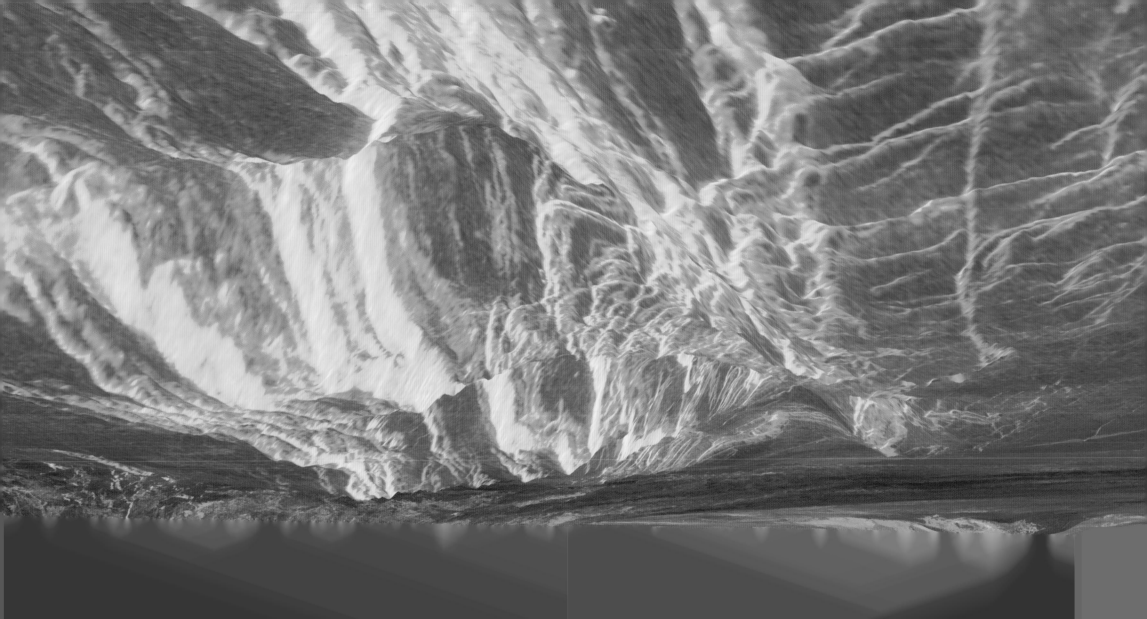

Venus: named after the Roman goddess of beauty and love. For a long time, our image of this neighbouring planet, also known as the Morning or Evening Star, was one tinged with romanticism. Yet various space missions such as Russia's Venera probes and America's Magellan have provided glimpses of a world which is anything but romantic, made up of volcanoes, craters, barren plains and temperatures in excess of 400 degrees, which would even cause metals to melt. How did Venus develop into this searingly hot, lethal environment while on Earth a life-friendly biosphere came into being? What happened on our sister planet, so similar to Earth in terms of size and mass? Some of the answers to that question should be provided by ESA's Venus Express probe. For, at present, the climatic catastrophe that befell Venus

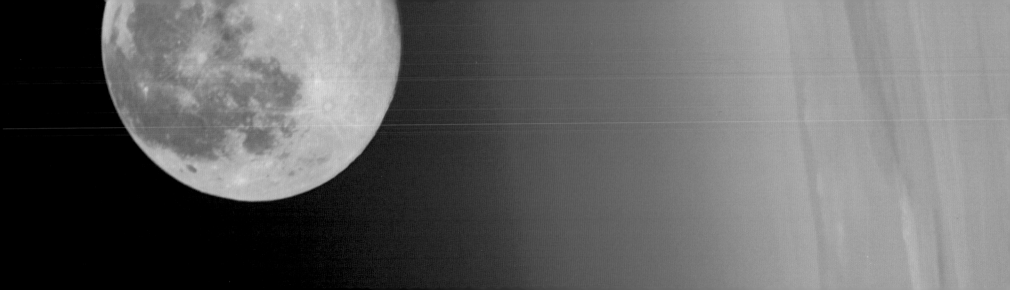

HEADING BACK TO THE MOON – WITH ION PROPULSION

Left: *the Moon, as seen by the crew of the International Space Station. Since the American Apollo Programme was discontinued in 1972, no astronaut has set foot on its surface. Now plans are being drawn up by both Americans and Europeans to return there. Studies are being carried out with a view to human missions whose intended destinations are first the Moon and then, in a few decades, even Mars. Robotic probes like Europe's SMART-1 – equipped with a futuristic ion propulsion system, laser communication equipment and other ground-breaking innovations – form part of these preparations.*

Right: *artist's impression of SMART-1.*

Following pages: *one of the first and last pictures taken during NASA's Apollo programme.* Left: *Edwin Aldrin on the Moon. In July 1969, Aldrin and Neil Armstrong were the first humans to set foot on the Earth's Moon. The image of these first steps taken on another world is one of the most famous of the 20th century.* Right: *Harrison H. Schmitt is photographed by Eugene A. Cernan performing a moonwalk. In 1972, these two Apollo 17 astronauts were the last spacefarers to set foot on the Moon. It now seems unlikely that they will be the last ever.*

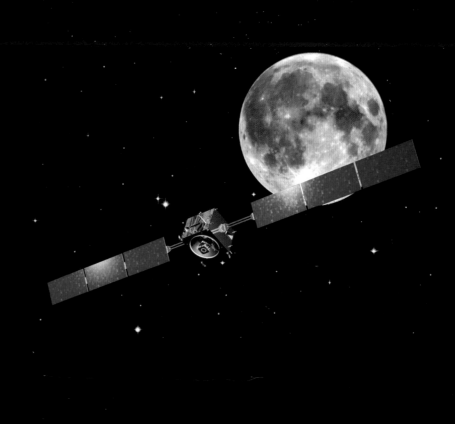

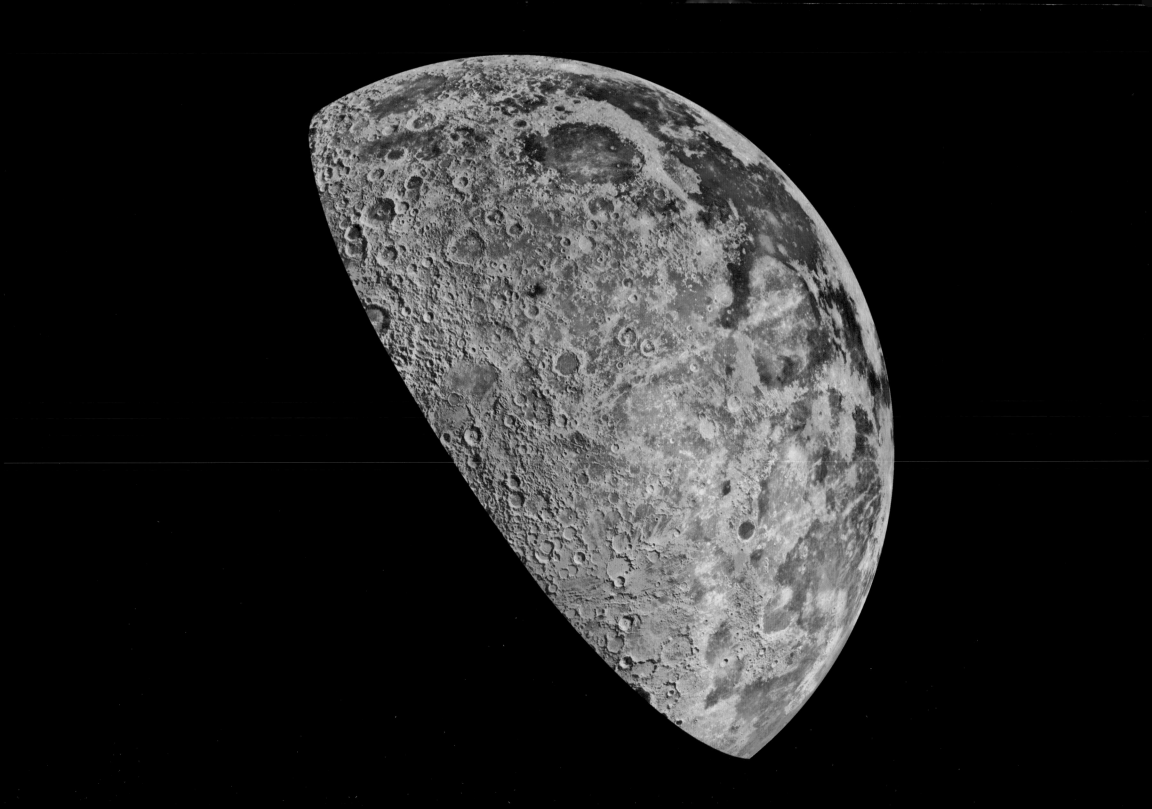

ETERNAL SHADOWS ON THE MOON

This false-colour image (left) taken by a German-American probe shows the composition of the Moon's surface. The deep blue colour indicates high levels of titanium. Yet, despite such robotic projects and the Apollo missions, many questions remain unanswered when it comes to lunar research. This is because it is now a number of years since the last probe flights and because astronauts always landed on the Moon's near side and even then, only close to its equator.

SMART-1 is now making a fresh attempt, investigating the Moon with the aid of instruments several times more sensitive than any previously used. For example, its infrared camera is capable of distinguishing between 256 instead of only 6 different wavelength ranges. In addition, mysterious areas of the Moon which are cloaked in eternal shadow, such as the floors of deep craters where water ice is suspected to exist, will be placed under the magnifying glass.

Right: *one of the first close-ups of the Moon sent back by SMART-1.*

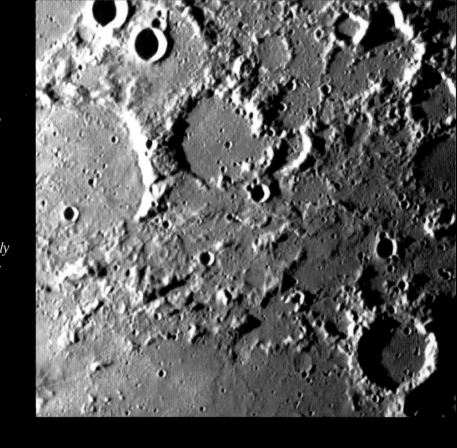

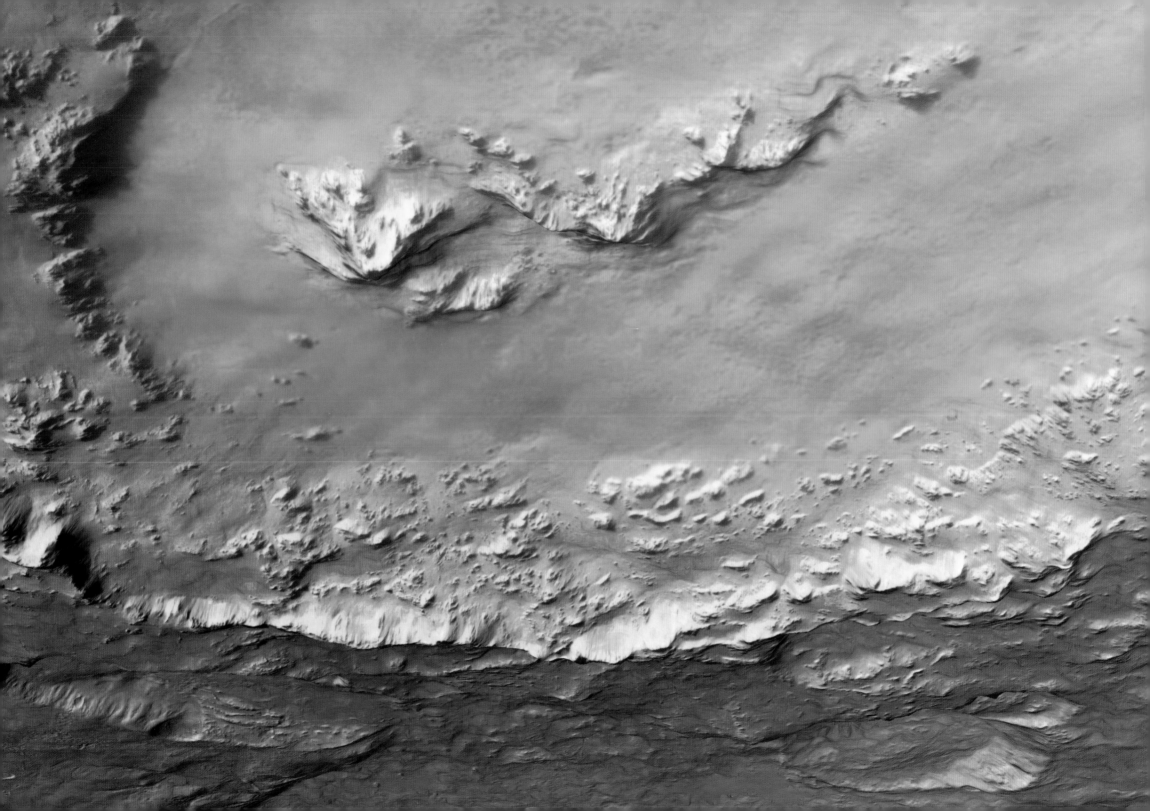

IS THERE OR WAS THERE EVER LIFE ON MARS?

Rarely has the constellation of Earth and Mars been as favourable as in 2003, when only six months were required to fly to the Red Planet. It was that opportunity which prompted the Earth's spacefaring nations to send a veritable flotilla of space probes on the 80 million kilometre journey to Mars. The most spectacular results were achieved by Europe's Mars Express mission and NASA's Rovers, Spirit and Opportunity.

The instruments carried on ESA's Mars Express probe were able to provide direct evidence of water ice at Mars's north and south poles and also found traces of methane in its atmosphere, a possible sign of the existence of simple life forms just below the Martian surface. That surface in turn was photographed with unparalleled clarity and precision by Europe's High Resolution Stereo Camera (HRSC), the raw data from which can provide brilliant colour images, computer-generated perspective views and stereo (3D) images. The NASA Rovers, meanwhile, analysed soil samples and sent back close-up pictures of the bizarre Martian landscape.

The picture to the left shows a perspective view of the Hale crater. This was calculated using data from the High Resolution Stereo Camera (HRSC) on board ESA's Mars Express probe.

ISLANDS IN THE DESERT

Following pages: table mountains in the desert, standing out like islands from a plain clearly formed at one time by water.

Below: artist's impression of Europe's Mars Express probe, carrying on board, among other instruments, the HRSC (High Resolution Stereo Camera). All the HRSC images in this book were produced in collaboration between Berlin's Freie Universität and the German space agency, the DLR. The copyright for all these images belongs to ESA, the DLR and Freie Universität Berlin (G. Neukum).

161

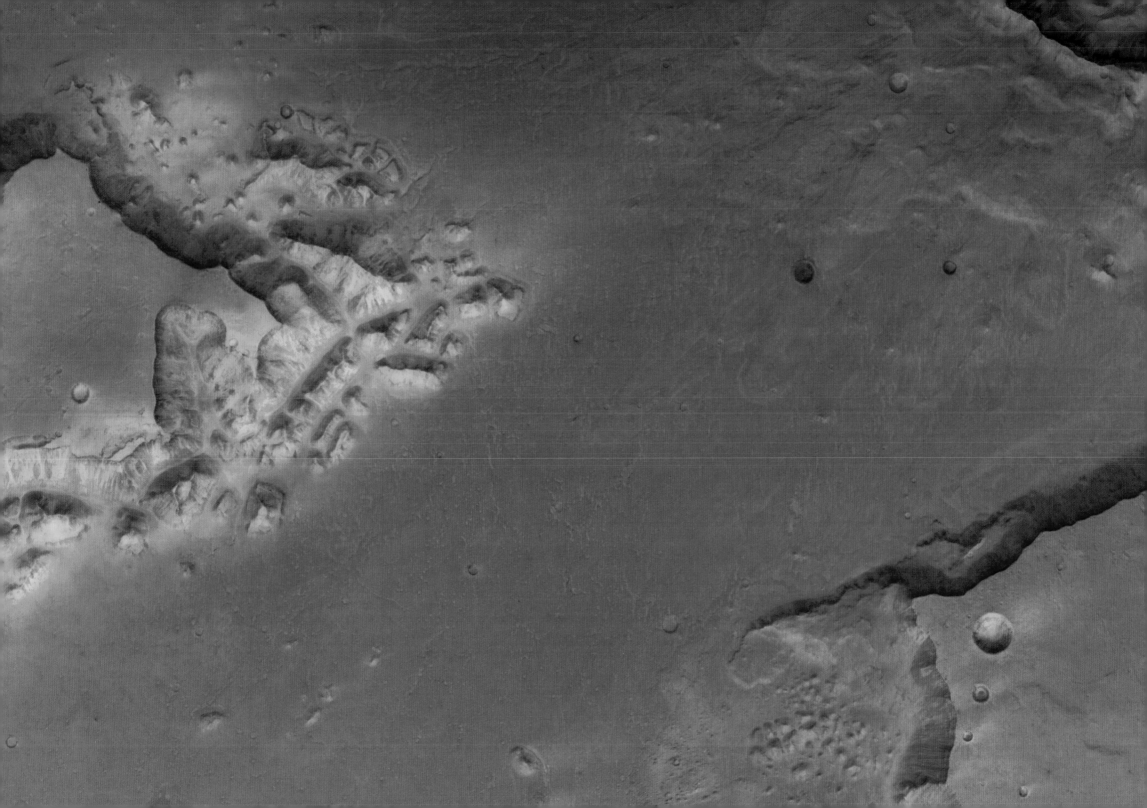

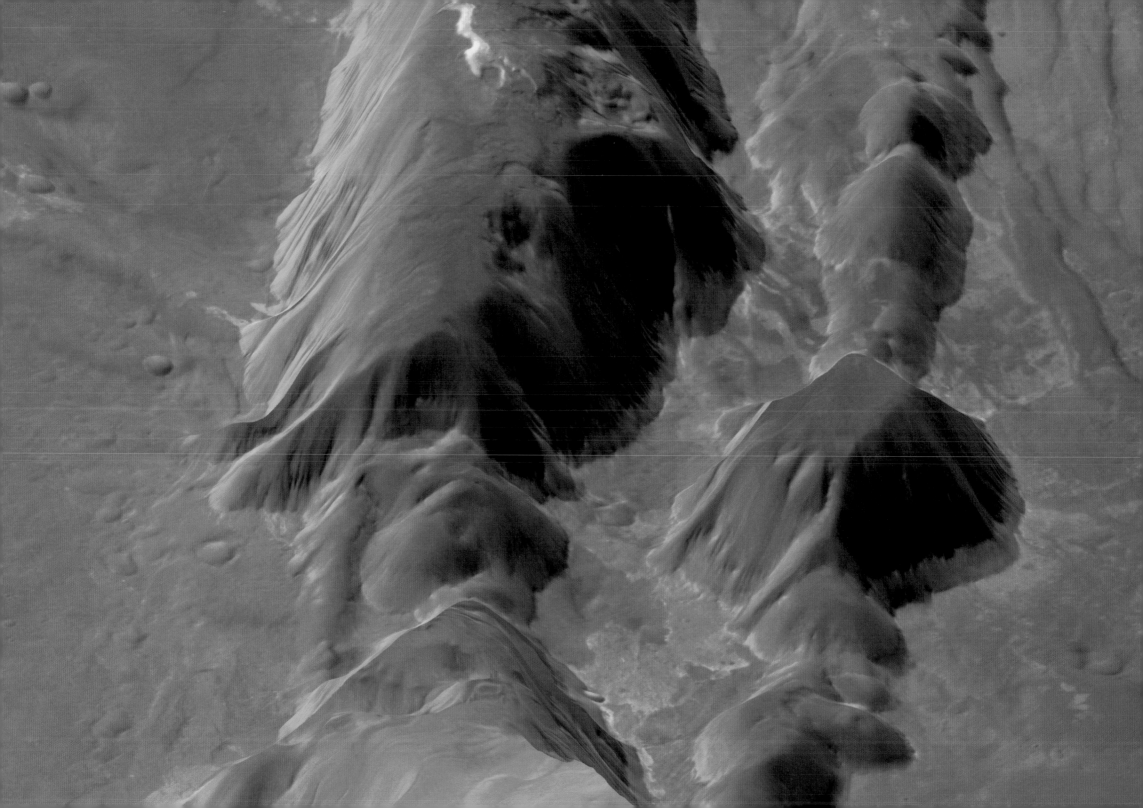

METHANE IN THE ATMOSPHERE

DECIPHERING IMAGES

In some respects Mars is very similar to Earth: our neighbouring planet also has seasons – although a Martian year is approximately twice as long as an Earth one – and, as the picture below shows, it even has a thin atmosphere with mist and clouds. Italian scientists participating in the Mars Express mission were even able to detect methane in the atmosphere, a discovery which raises new questions, since this gas could also point to the presence of simple life forms.

Following pages, left: *the Solis Planum region. By "deciphering" such images of spectacular landscapes, planetary researchers can learn more about the past of Mars and of our Solar System. This image shows craters which were clearly not formed by volcanic activity but as a result of meteorite impacts and trenches attributable to tectonic shifts.*
Following pages, right: *similar phenomena can be seen in the Acheron Fossae region, shown here in a perspective view.*

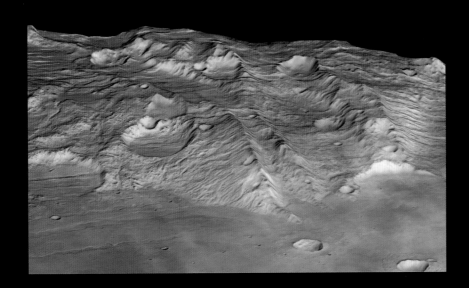

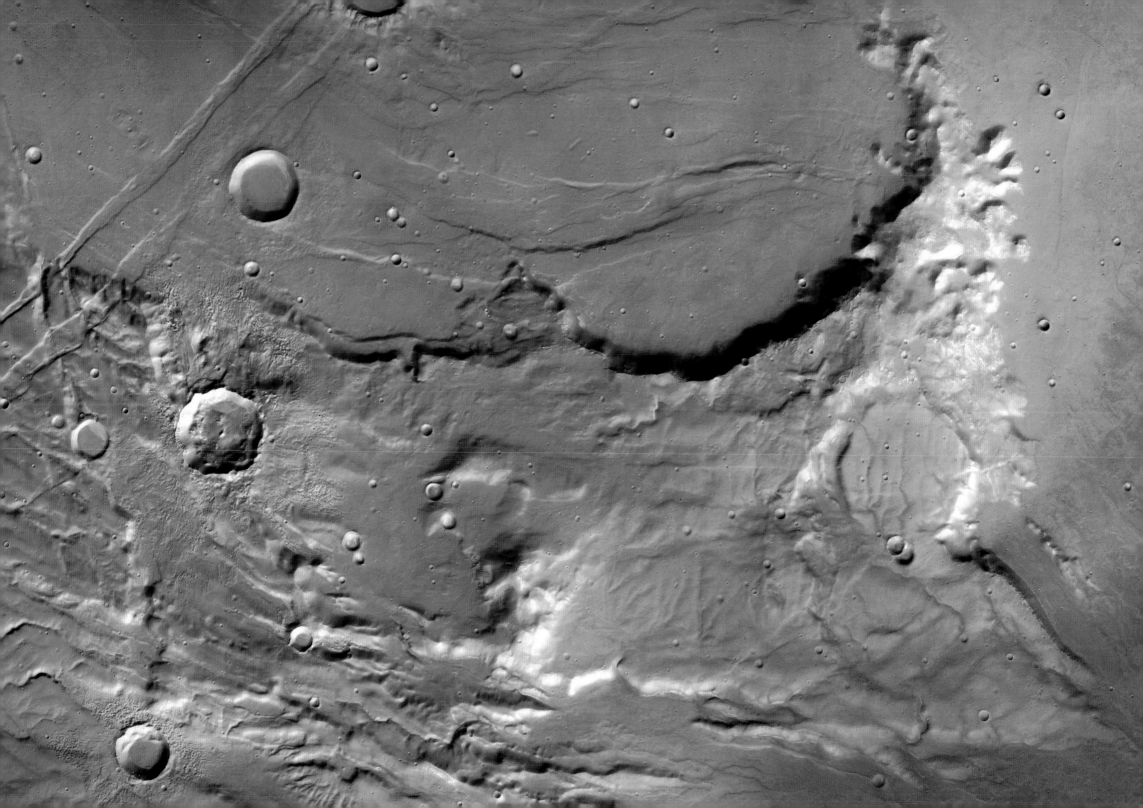

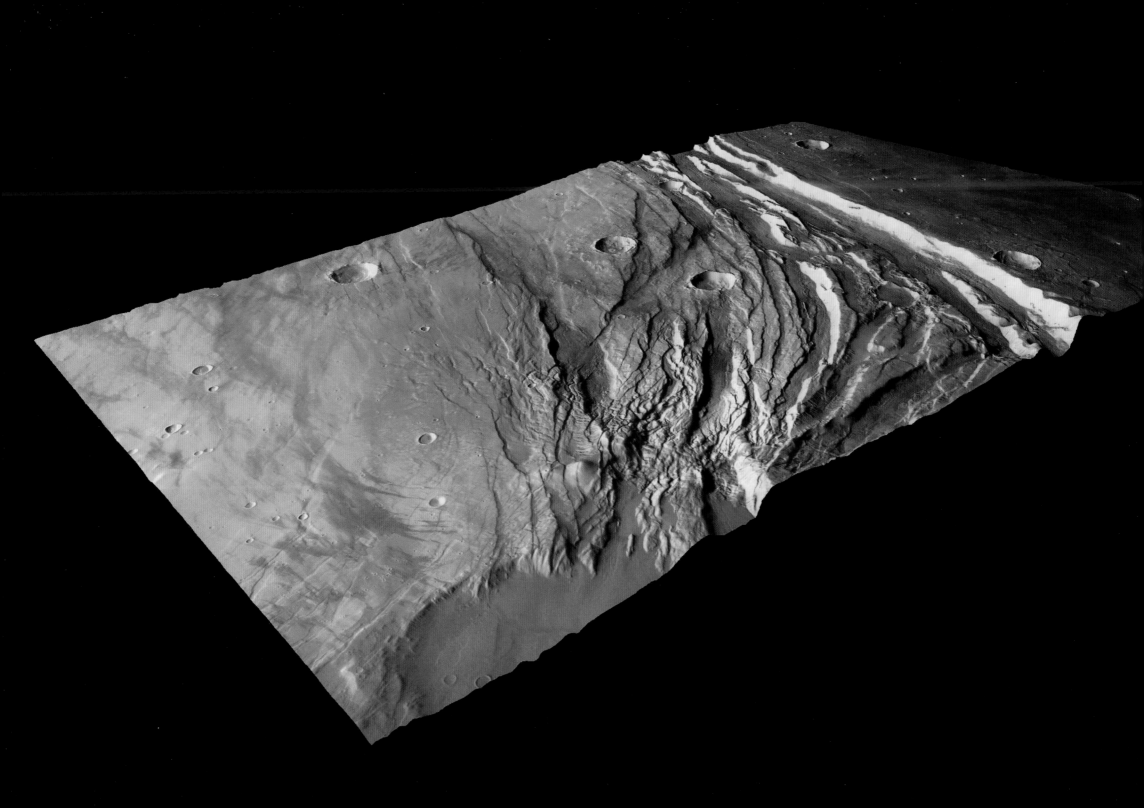

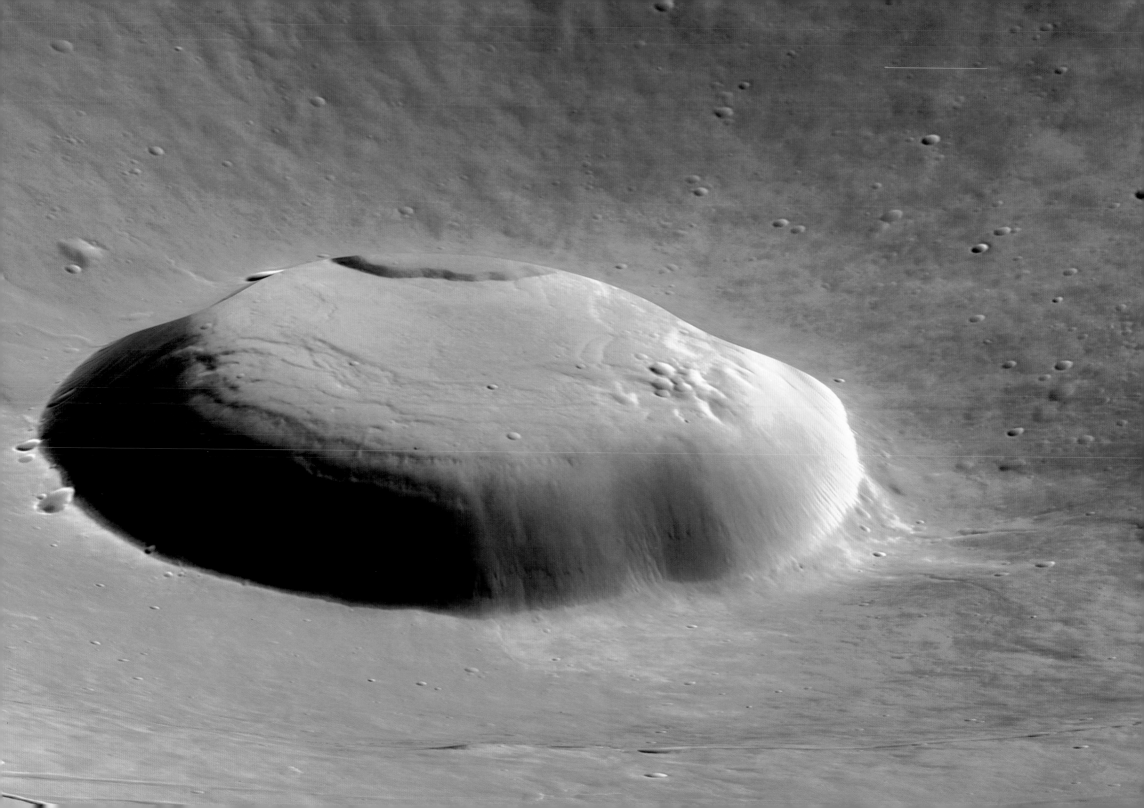

A "WATERFALL" MADE OF SAND

The Albor Tholus volcano or, to be more precise, its cauldron-shaped crater or caldera. Apart from the unusual fact that the crater is almost as deep as the entire volcano is high, it was something else entirely about this picture that amazed scientists: the "waterfall" pouring sand from the edge of the crater into its depths. Since Mars has an atmosphere, it too has storms that can give rise to such sand drifts, something that could not occur on the Moon, for example.

169

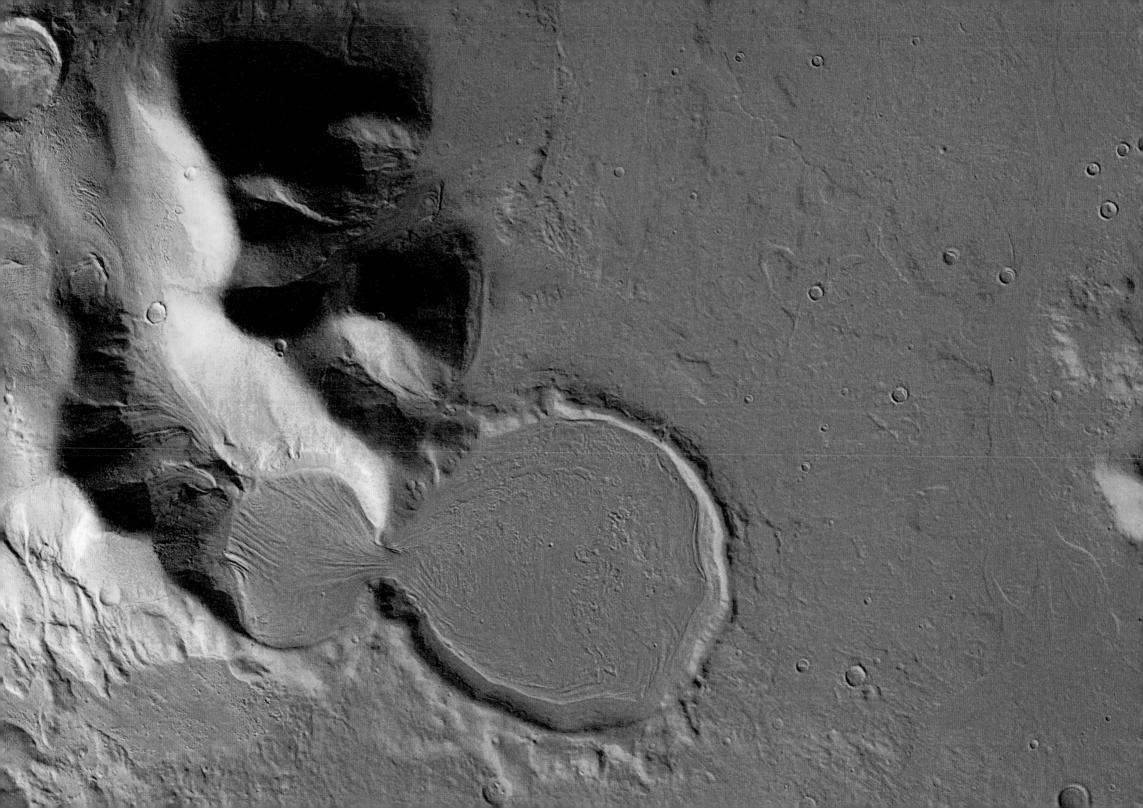

DISCOVERED: A SEA ON THE DESERT PLANET

This HRSC image from ESA's Mars Express probe (above right) caused a major sensation. Massive ice floes are visible on the frozen sea, estimated to be 50 metres in depth and as big as the North Sea. Perhaps this discovery will provide crucial clues to questions which are still to be conclusively answered, such as why our neighbouring planet, on which huge expanses of water, rivers and even oceans had clearly once formed, was transformed into an arid red planet, and where its water might have gone. The existing evidence indicates that it did not all evaporate into space, but that, instead some was preserved in permafrost on and under the Martian surface.
Below right: *this perspective view shows water ice at Mars's north pole. Previously, French scientists had established with the help of Mars Express data that the ice caps at Mars's south pole consisted of frozen water.*

Left: *this Martian landscape was clearly shaped by the action of glaciers millions of years ago.*

Following pages: *this valley, which forms part of the Valles Marineris trench system, is called Tithonium Chasma. Studies of its surface of craters, trenches and sediment deposits also point to the conclusion that Mars must have experienced dramatic climate change.*

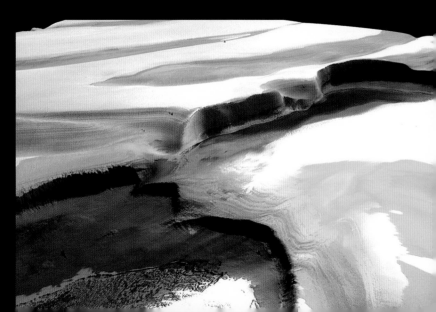

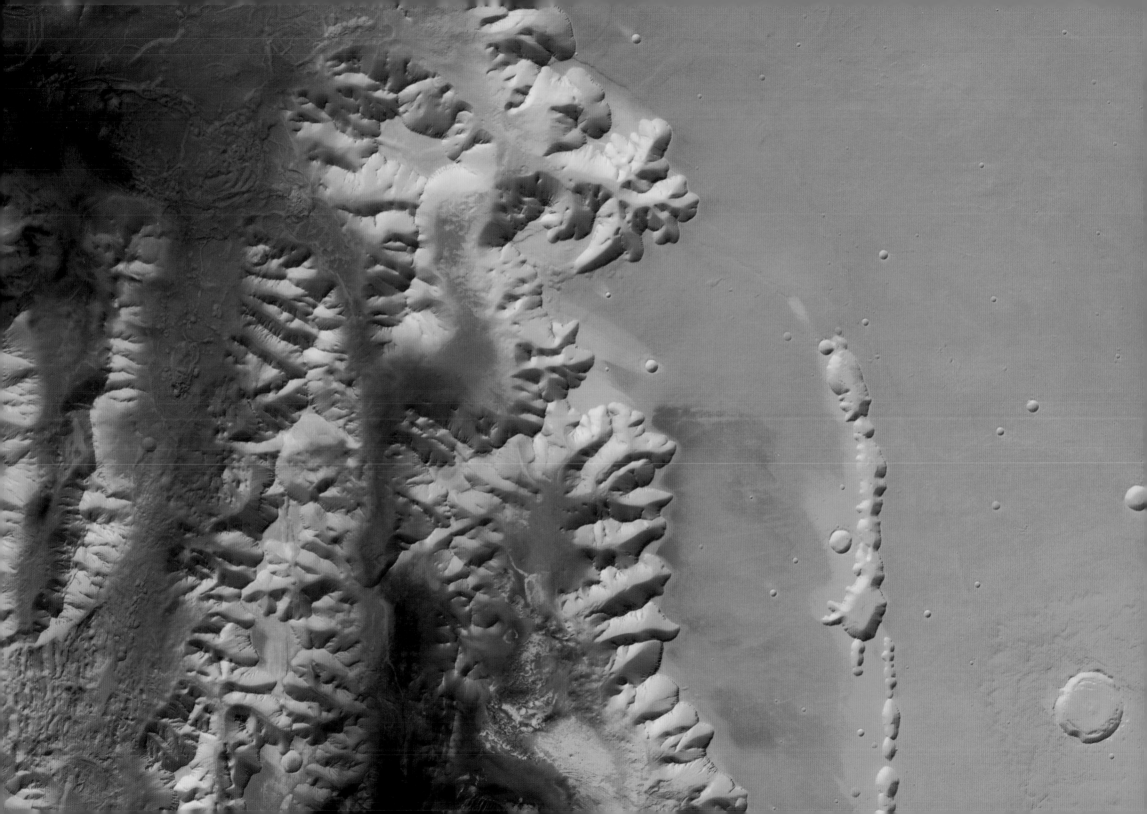

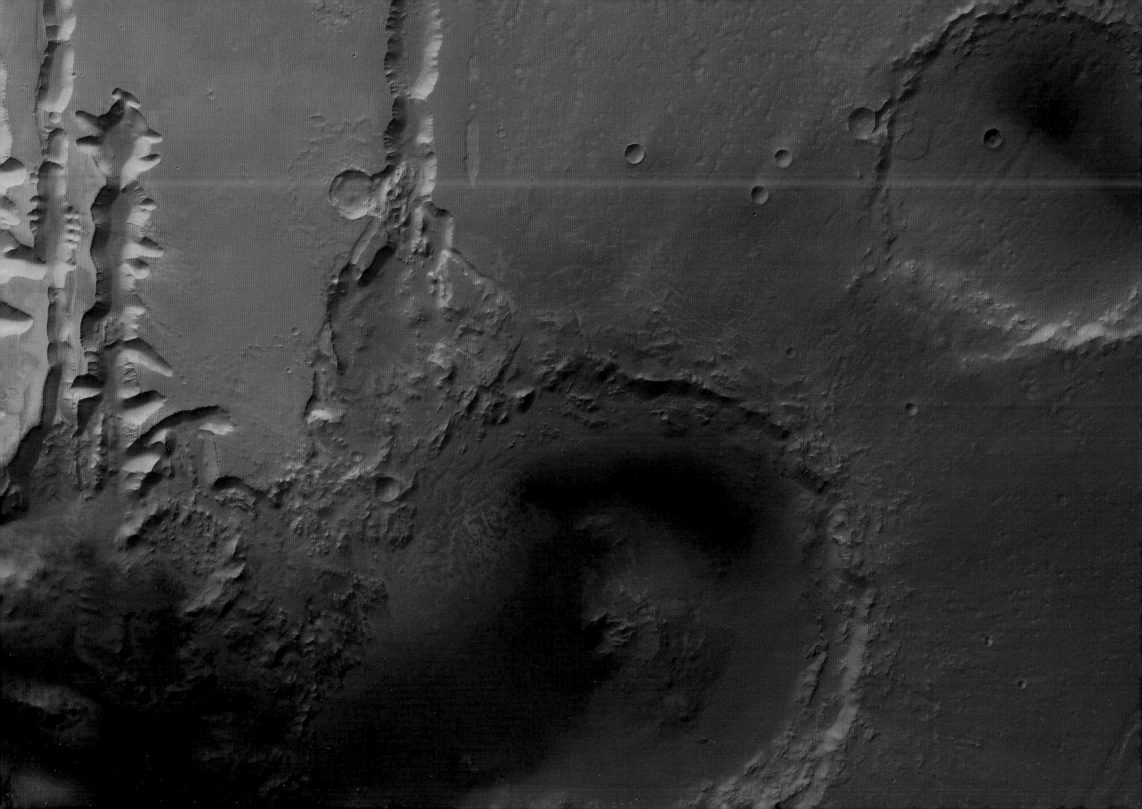

THE BLUEBERRY MYSTERY

Since the beginning of 2004, the NASA Rovers Spirit and Opportunity have been busy making tracks across the red sands of Mars. On the left is a false colour image of Martian rock taken by Opportunity, which surprised scientists so much that they have been puzzling over the strange spherical deposits at great length. Such formations can arise due to a range of geological processes, one possible explanation being the cooling of lava. However, for the time being, it is thought that moisture present in the rock played a role in the formation of these mysterious objects. Could it be that these "droplets" measuring just a few millimetres across, and christened "blueberries" by scientists, constitute further evidence of the presence of water on Mars?

Right: *the mysterious "blueberry" formations in close-up.*

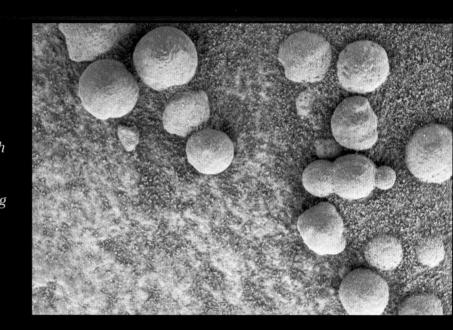

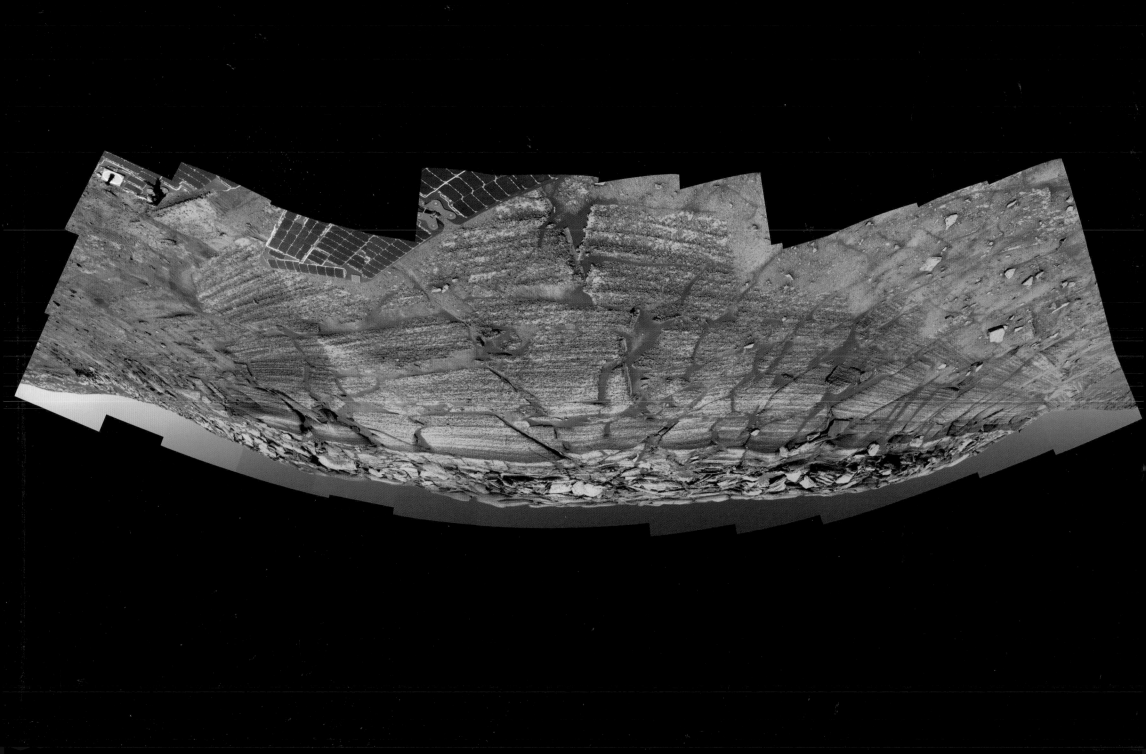

ROCKY CLUES TO THE MARTIAN PUZZLE

Left: *the Martian landscape as seen by the Mars Rover Opportunity: scientists believe the cracks in this rock formation to have been created by water forcing its way in and then freezing. Thus, little by little, the tiniest clues are gradually helping to solve the puzzle surrounding the presence of water and life on Mars. Nevertheless, further missions to Mars will be necessary if these fundamental questions are to be cleared up once and for all. NASA and ESA are already preparing for further missions, including others using rovers and probes intended to return rock samples to Earth.*

Above right: *dunes on Mars – a false-colour image sent back by Mars Rover Opportunity.*
Below right: *a false-colour image showing the landing site of the Spirit Rover. The colours make it easier to distinguish between "clean" and dust-covered stones and between darker and lighter sections. Such pictures were used to determine the Rover's subsequent direction of travel and which of the rocks and stones in the vicinity to examine.*

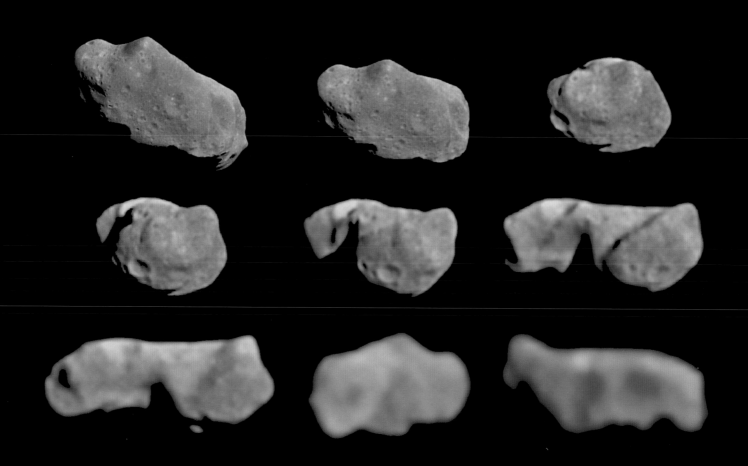

Between Mars and the orbit of the giant planet, Jupiter, lies some half a billion kilometres of empty space; empty that is save for the thousands upon thousands of chunks of rock, most only a few kilometres across, that form a vast rocky belt. Either they are the remains of a former planet smashed into pieces in a collision or, more probably, the dust from which all heavenly bodies were once formed, in this instance never compressing to form a planet. Instead, the tidal forces exerted over a great distance by Jupiter, with its enormous mass, have ensured that they remain fragments.

Main picture, left: *false-colour views of the asteroid Ida seen from various perspectives and distances. The picture of Ida, below left, came as a big surprise to scientists since it showed that even this small asteroid is orbited by its own moon – in this case a chunk of rock 1.5 kilometres across.*

Asteroids attract so much attention because of the potential threat they pose to the Earth, even though they only cross its path very rarely.

Below: *two craters in Canada caused by impacts from a pair of asteroids.*

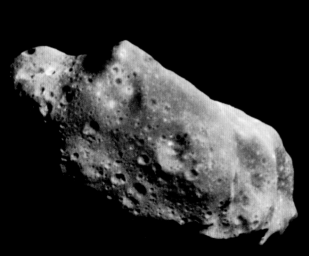

RENDEZVOUS WITH A DIRTY SNOWBALL

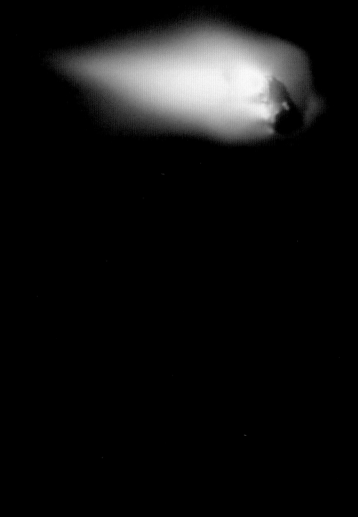

Every 75 to 77 years Halley's Comet, following an eccentric trajectory, comes shooting out of the depths of the universe and into our Solar System. The last time this occurred was in 1986, when the comet with its glowing tail (see main picture, left) provided a magnificent sight in the night sky. The scientific world, meanwhile, was presented with a rare opportunity to study this "dirty snowball" made up of ice and minerals in greater detail. To that end, the European Space Agency, ESA had sent its Giotto probe on its way some months before. In March 1986, Giotto came within 600 kilometres of the comet, sending back data and images to Earth (including the picture on the right). For the first time, people were able to set eyes on the actual core of a comet.

More recently, the United States and Europe once again dispatched probes to hunt for comets. While NASA's "Deep Impact" probe successfully shot a large projectile into a comet's core and performed chemical analysis on the resulting ejected material (or ejecta), ESA's Rosetta probe is actually planning to land a small research station on the surface of one. The results of these unique missions are expected to provide us with information on our cosmic origins, given that the original matter from which all celestial bodies in the Solar System, including the Earth, were once formed is preserved in comets almost unchanged. By examining them, therefore, we are in a sense able to witness the birth of our very own world and embark on a fantastic journey back to our very origins, when our planet was formed out of a cosmic dust cloud.

Left: *Jupiter, photographed by the two-part Cassini-Huygens probe, a joint project involving NASA, ESA and ASI, the Italian space agency. The picture was taken as the probe flew by on its way to Saturn. The giant planet has a turbulent atmosphere, visible here as swirling bands of cloud. Visible to the left of Jupiter is Io, one of the so-called inner moons.*

Jupiter is the colossus of the planets in our Solar System. Its mass is twice that of all the other eight planets put together, and even 300 Earths would not outweigh it. And that, despite the fact that it is a gas planet and therefore does not have a solid surface. Its gas masses simply become increasingly dense the nearer they are to its centre. Jupiter, like the Sun, consists mainly of hydrogen and helium. Yet despite having the nuclear fuel at its disposal that causes stars to shine, it lacks the critical mass required to trigger an atomic chain reaction. Although it does not quite have what it takes to be a sun, Jupiter, with its 40 or so moons, is practically a solar system in minia-ture. In the picture to the right, Io can be seen casting its shadow on to the giant planet.

Following pages, left: *the "Great Red Spot" as seen by NASA's Voyager 1 probe. This violent hurricane – considerably larger than the Earth – was first sighted more than 300 years ago.*
Following pages, right: *polar lights at Jupiter's north pole recorded by the Hubble Space Telescope, jointly operated by NASA and ESA.*

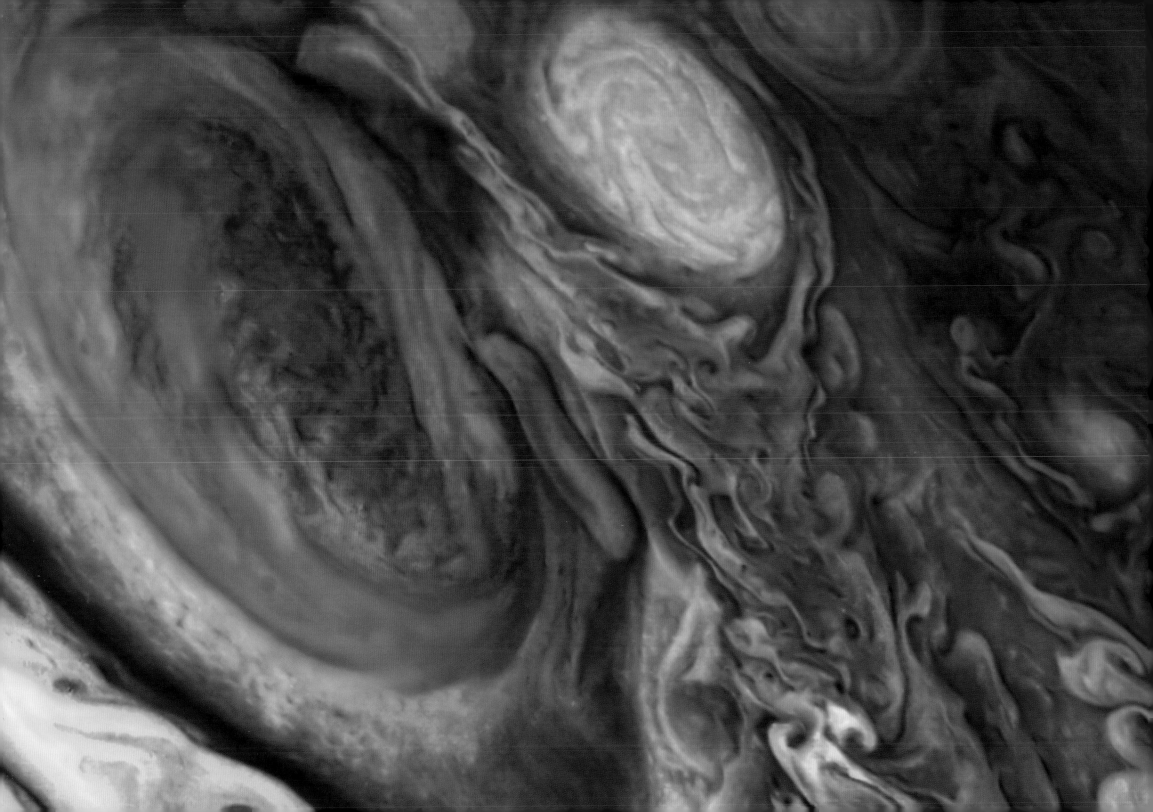

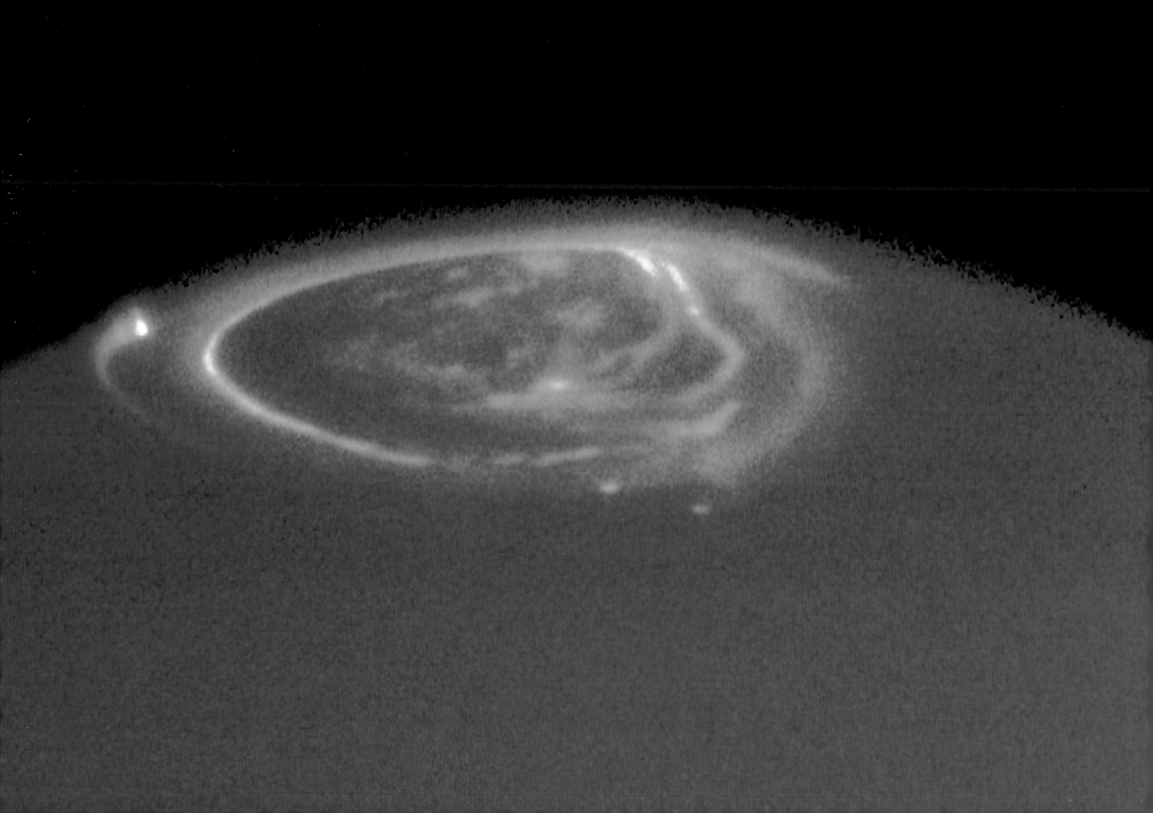

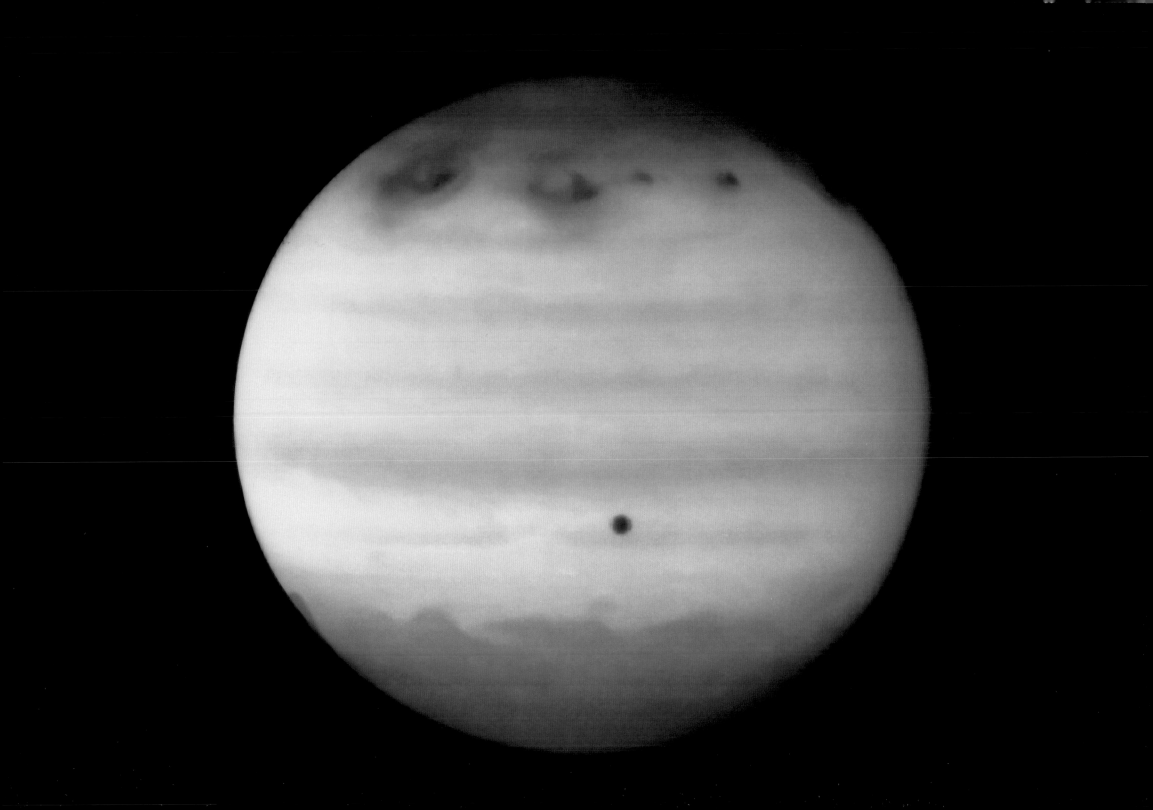

EYEWITNESSES TO A COSMIC COLLISION

VOLCANIC IO AND ICY EUROPA

On 18th July 1994, as fragments of comet Shoemaker-Levy hurtled towards Jupiter, scientists the world over trained their telescopes on the point where this spectacular event was about to take place and prepared to witness the imminent cosmic collision. At various points in their existence, all of the planets and moons in the Solar System must have experienced impacts of this kind. This time, however, for the first time the opportunity was there to observe the event live, as it happened. For the first time, humans would be able to observe an impact of the type that all the planets and moons in the Solar System must have repeatedly experienced since coming into being. The scientific world was not to be disappointed. The Hubble Telescope, for example, delivered the ultraviolet image on the left, which clearly shows the multiple impacts to the bottom of the picture. As an added bonus, Jupiter's moon, Io is once again visible, this time in the upper half of the picture.

Small image below: *comet fragments hurtling towards Jupiter. Before impact, the comet was broken up due to the powerful force of attraction exerted by the giant planet.*

Following pages: *the volcanic moon, Io* (left), *and another of Jupiter's moons, Europa* (right). *Both pictures were sent back by a German-American probe, which had been observing Jupiter's moons for a number of years. Dark patches are visible on the icy surface of Europa which resemble a slowly melting ice surface (and not purely by coincidence). Scientists suspect there to be an ocean of liquid water under the frozen surface, which could possibly even be home to simple life forms.*

187

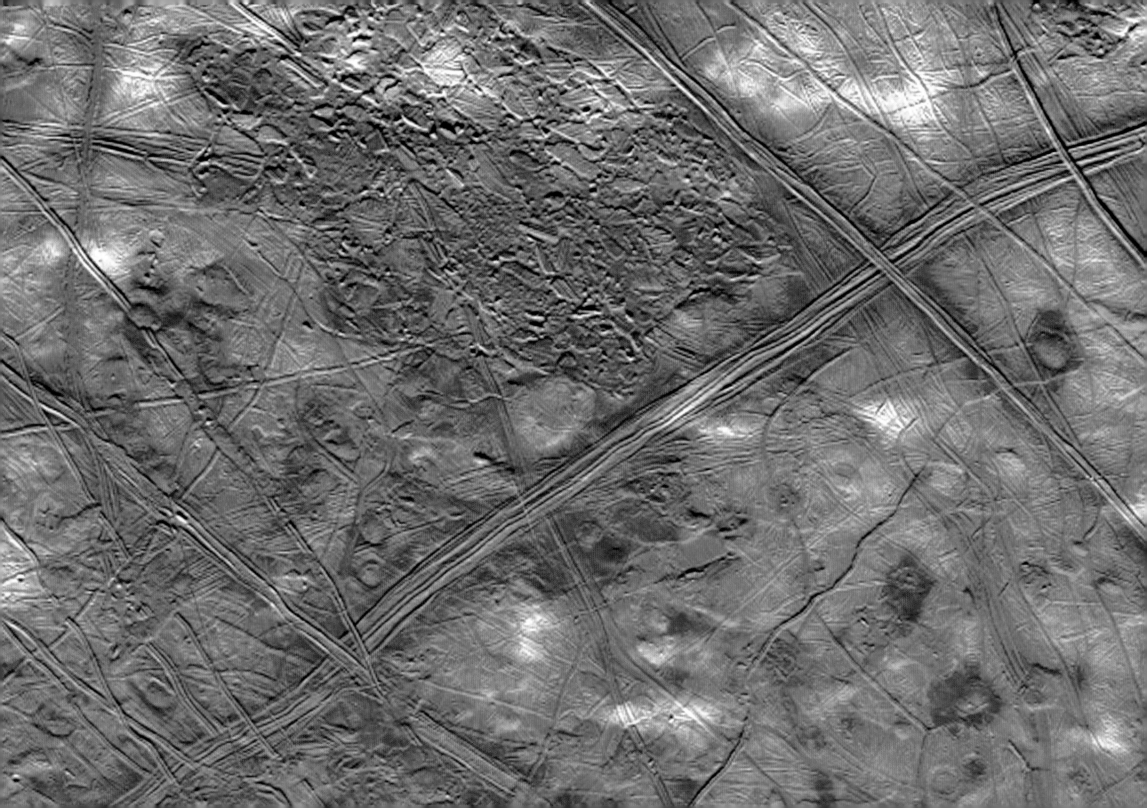

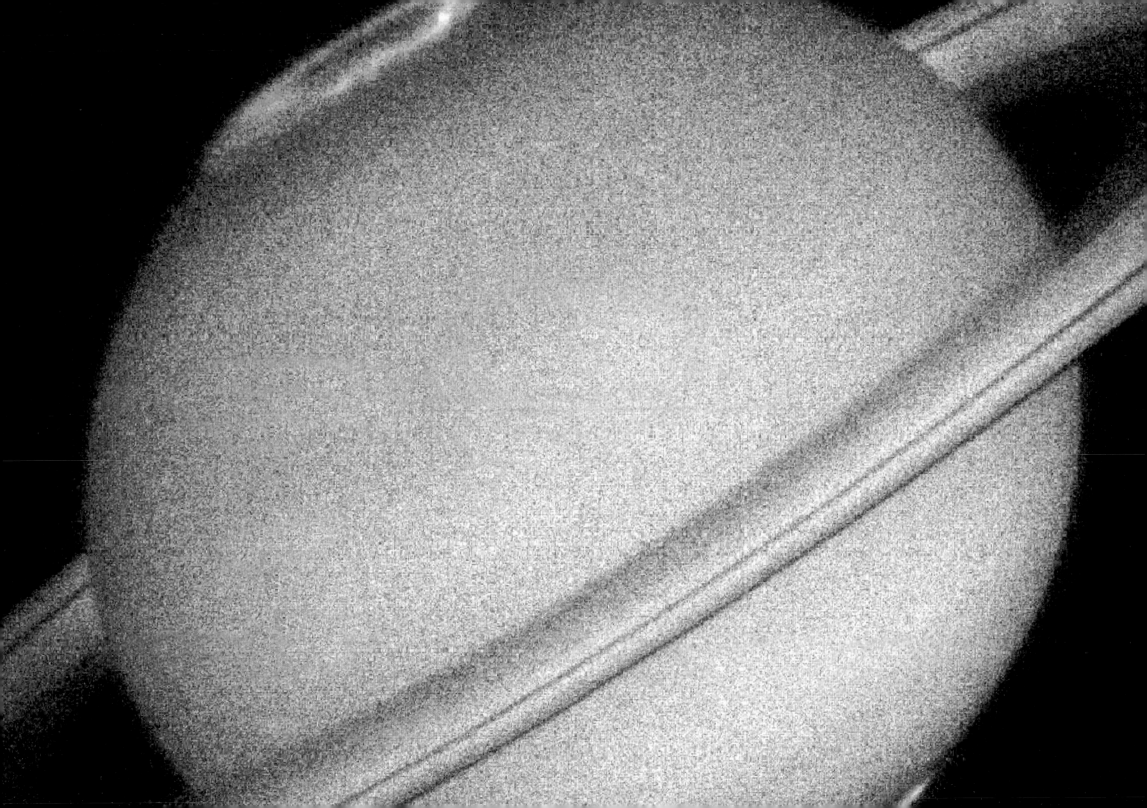

IS MAJESTY, THE LORD OF THE RINGS

aturn, sometimes known as the "Lord of the Rings" is perhaps the
ost beautiful of all the planets. It orbits the Sun at a distance of over
 billion kilometres from the Earth, accompanied on its way by myriad
oons. Although the other large planets in the outer Solar System are
lso circled by a delicate band of rings, none can rival Saturn for sheer
ajesty. Also, from a scientific perspective, the Saturn system, and
bove all its moon Titan, are of particular interest. Titan, the second
iggest moon in the entire Solar System, even outstrips the planets
luto and Mercury in size, and is the only moon enveloped in a dense
tmosphere. That is why American and European scientists chose the
inged planet and its moons, especially Titan, as the destination of one
f the most ambitious space missions of all time, and sent the Cassini-
luygens probe on a voyage halfway across the Solar System.

Main picture, left: *Saturn with auroras, also known as polar lights.*

light: *artist's impression of Cassini-Huygens, a joint endeavour between
JASA, ESA and the Italian Space Agency ASI*

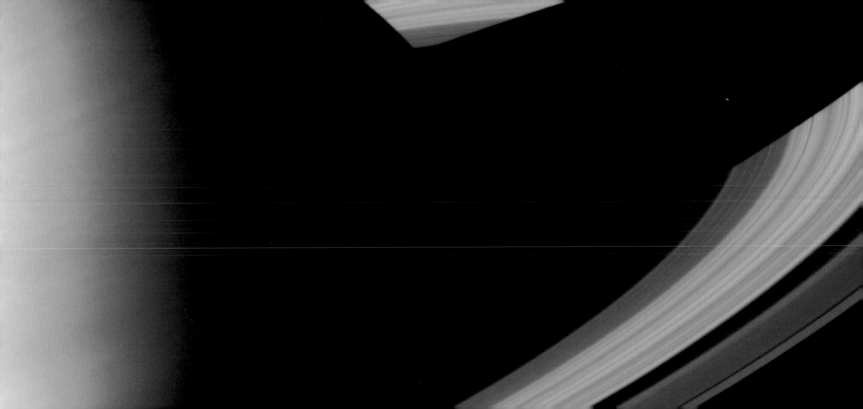

FLYBY SNAPSHOTS

For seven years, the US-built mother-craft Cassini had given the smaller European probe Huygens a piggy-back ride on its way to Saturn. Upon arrival, Cassini sent back the first images of the gas planet, its rings and moons. On its way to Titan, Cassini-Huygens also flew by several of Saturn's other moons.

Main picture, left: *Saturn.*

Right: *the Phoebe moon seen from Cassini-Huygens. The picture was taken from a distance of 13,000 kilometres. Scientists are still puzzling over the exact composition of this small celestial body, which clearly contains far more chemical elements than was previously assumed. The surface seems to consist of water ice mixed with various minerals, as is to be found in clay and loam deposits on Earth. All of which indicates that Phoebe was not formed at the same time as Saturn, but that it previously described its trajectory much further out on the edge of the Solar System and that it was only later that it was captured by the force of attraction exerted by the ringed planet.*

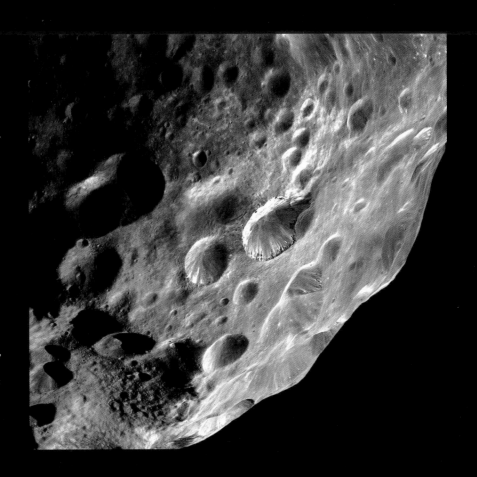

193

RINGS OF DUST AND ICE

Ultraviolet images of Saturn's rings taken by Cassini's on-board camera. The turquoise colour indicates ice, while red points to rocky particles. The pictures were taken at the end of 2004, shortly before the two probes went their separate ways. While Cassini continued to investigate the Saturn system, Huygens's course was calculated to make it head straight for Titan before plunging into its atmosphere in a spectacular finale to its seven-year journey through space.

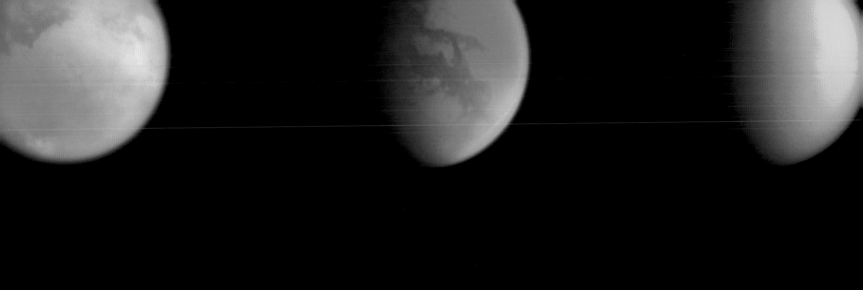

A JOURNEY INTO THE PAST

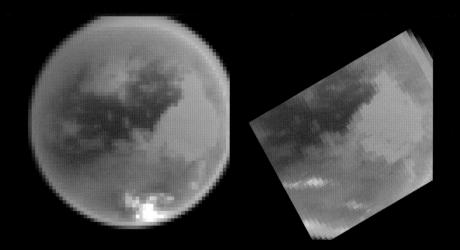

Titan is the most mysterious of all the Solar System moons. Why, unlike other moons, including Jupiter's even bigger satellite Ganymede, for example, does it have an atmosphere? What lies under the thick blanket of cloud which masks its surface? In fact, what makes Titan so special is that the chemical composition of its atmosphere clearly resembles that of the infant Earth before life was able to take hold on our planet. Titan is thus an ideal candidate for the study of fundamental questions such as the origins of life. In a sense, therefore, the Cassini-Huygens mission is also a journey back in time into the Earth's past to witness the early stages of life.

Main picture, left: *the left-hand image shows Titan as it appears to the naked eye, as a diffusely shimmering yellowish sphere. Luckily modern sensors are able to see through its atmosphere, with the result that in the middle and right-hand images even individual continents are visible.*

In addition, both of the infrared images (above right) prove that variations in weather conditions occur on Titan. The right-hand picture shows clouds not visible on the other photograph taken a few days earlier.

14th January 2005 was destined to become a great day for space exploration. Since its separation from NASA's Cassini spacecraft, ESA's Huygens research capsule had been on course for Titan. The riskiest part of the mission still lay ahead: entry into the dense atmosphere, followed, it was hoped, by a soft landing on the surface of this mysterious moon.

But questions remained over the probe's ability to survive the journey into a completely unknown world. In ESA's Space Operations Centre in Darmstadt, Germany, experts waited with bated breath for a sign of life from Huygens. And then, from a distance of a billion kilometres, the probe began sending back to Earth the first data on the chemical composition of Titan's atmosphere, even following this up later with images of its surface. Huygens had coped successfully with the critical phase of atmospheric entry (see artist's impression, left) and, with parachutes slowing its speed down from over 20,000 to only 20 kilometres per hour, landed intact on the moon's surface. It had successfully achieved the first ever landing on a celestial body in the outer Solar System:

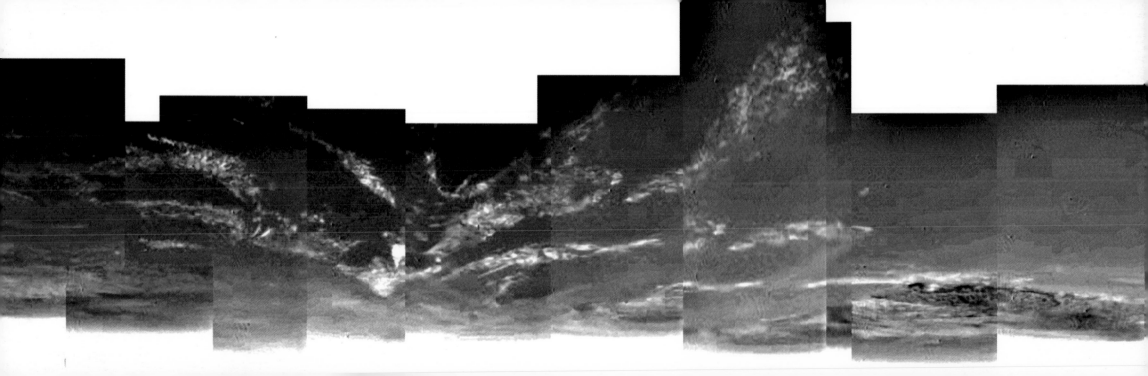

RIVERS OF METHANE AT MINUS 170 DEGREES

Never before had either Earth-based telescopes or space probes been able to catch a glimpse of the surface of Saturn's mysterious Titan moon. The pictures transmitted by Huygens showed a strange vista of land masses and seas, visible in the aerial photographs (left) taken during the probe's descent. A deeply fissured landscape in which, with temperatures at 170 degrees below zero, streams and rivers run with liquid methane. And even after landing, the probe continued to transmit data: lumps of what is clearly frozen material can be seen in the midst of a barren plain (right). For many years to come, scientists will continue to evaluate the data from this mission, possibly comparable in importance to the first landing of a probe on Mars and perhaps even the first astronaut flights to the Moon under NASA's Apollo Programme.

CALLING ALL EXTRATERRESTRIALS

FLIGHT INTO INFINITY

The outer planets Uranus (main picture, left), Neptune and tiny Pluto have barely been explored. Only NASA's two Voyager probes, in flights lasting several decades, have flown by the big gas planets, Uranus and Neptune. Unlike with Mars, the distances are too great to regularly send probes to these planets, given that they are situated several billion kilometres away from us. The Voyager probes took more than ten years to even be able to photograph these two planets from a distance. They have now left the Solar System and continue to send signals back to Earth. Should they be discovered by other civilisations at some point in the distant future, they carry on board a wealth of information and messages: photographs of the Earth and its landscapes, X-ray images of the human body and tape recordings of sounds such as a baby crying and Bach's Fugues, as well as sentences spoken by people from many different lands. While some of these contain invitations to make contact, others, such as this one, are more cautious: "We are happy here. May you be happy where you are".

Below: *Neptune, photographed by Voyager 2. This planet has the most violent storms in the entire Solar System with wind speeds in excess of 2,000 kilometres per hour.*

Following pages: *Voyager 2's last picture of Neptune and its moon, Triton. Both Voyager probes have now left the Solar System to continue on their endless journeys.*

203

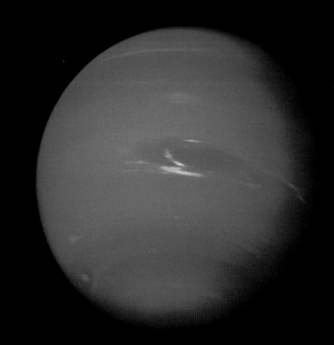

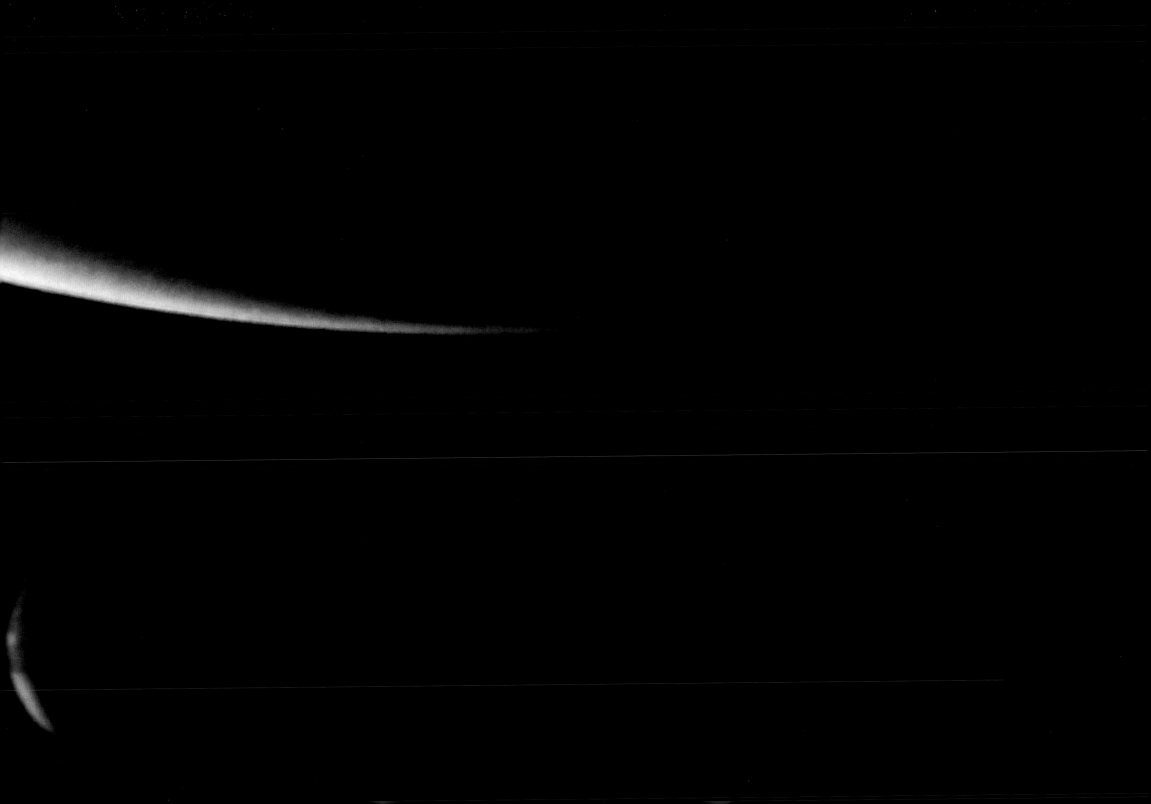

3D IMAGES OF THE RED PLANET

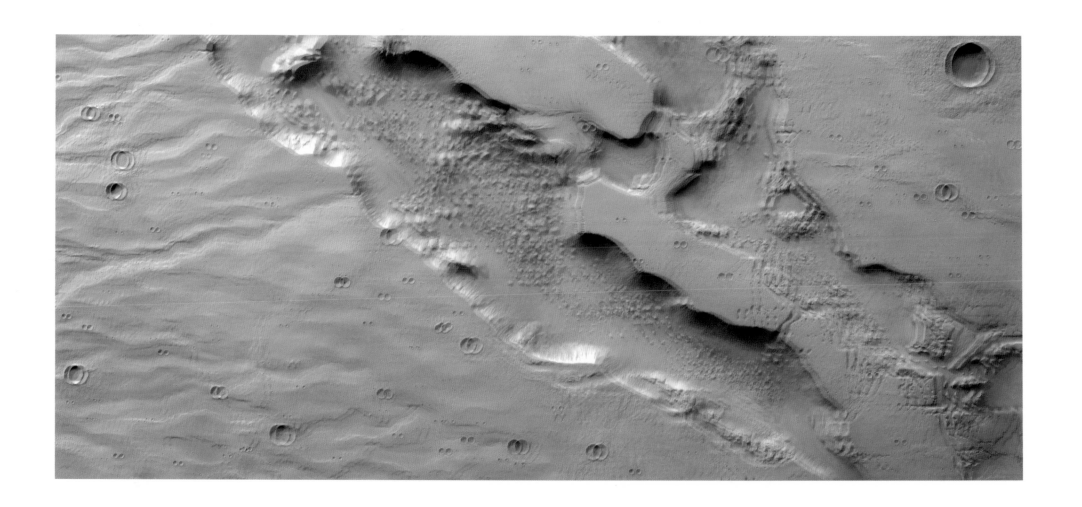

3D IMAGES OF THE RED PLANET

The pictures sent to Earth by Europe's Mars Express probe are quite unique, not least in terms of their precision. Due to their high resolution and the colour information they convey, they show details of the Martian surface which have provided scientists with entirely new insights, enabling them to reach conclusions about past events on the Red Planet.

These images become all the more informative once the data have been processed to produce three-dimensional views. These 3D or "stereo" images reveal the topography of what is a truly spectacular landscape: where it was thought there would be high plateaus, instead the images show uneven terrain and trenches. The slopes of volcanoes fall away into depths, the like of which is unknown on Earth. Such stereo images are thus providing scientists with a new perspective on Mars, but they also give non-scientists a real impression of the physical appearance of our neighbouring planet, since through them they are able to take a virtual tour of its surface.

To obtain a 3D effect, put on the stereoscopic glasses enclosed with this book, ensuring that the red lens is positioned to the left.

Left: these valleys on Mars (Dao Valles and Niger Valles) are more than 2,000 metres deep.

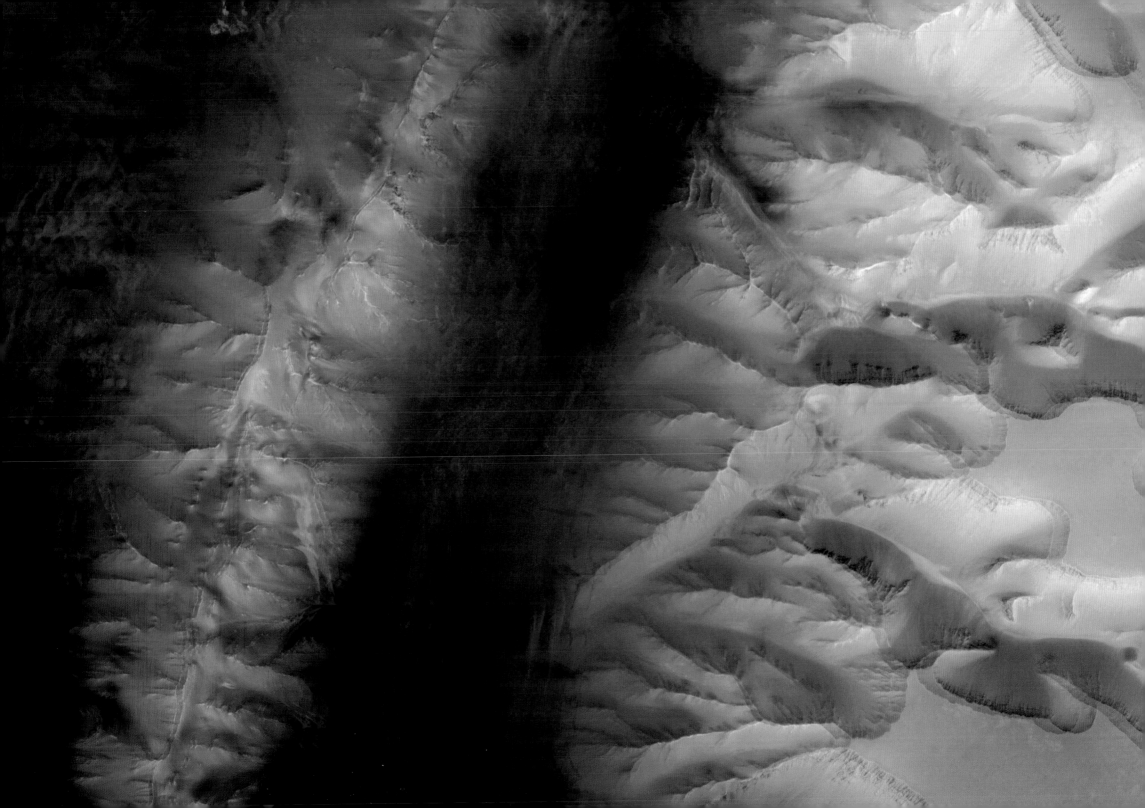

A TURBULENT PAST

Left: *immense canyon systems clearly formed by the action of water and wind. Following pages, overleaf: an impact crater caused by a meteorite strike. Stereo images such as these tell us a great deal about Mars's turbulent past. Thus, for example, the central peak in the middle of the crater pictured overleaf was shaped by the force of the impact, which first compressed the mass of rock before, as it were, allowing it to "bounce back". The crater edge itself, on the other hand, is made up of material ejected into the surrounding area as the meteorite struck.* 211

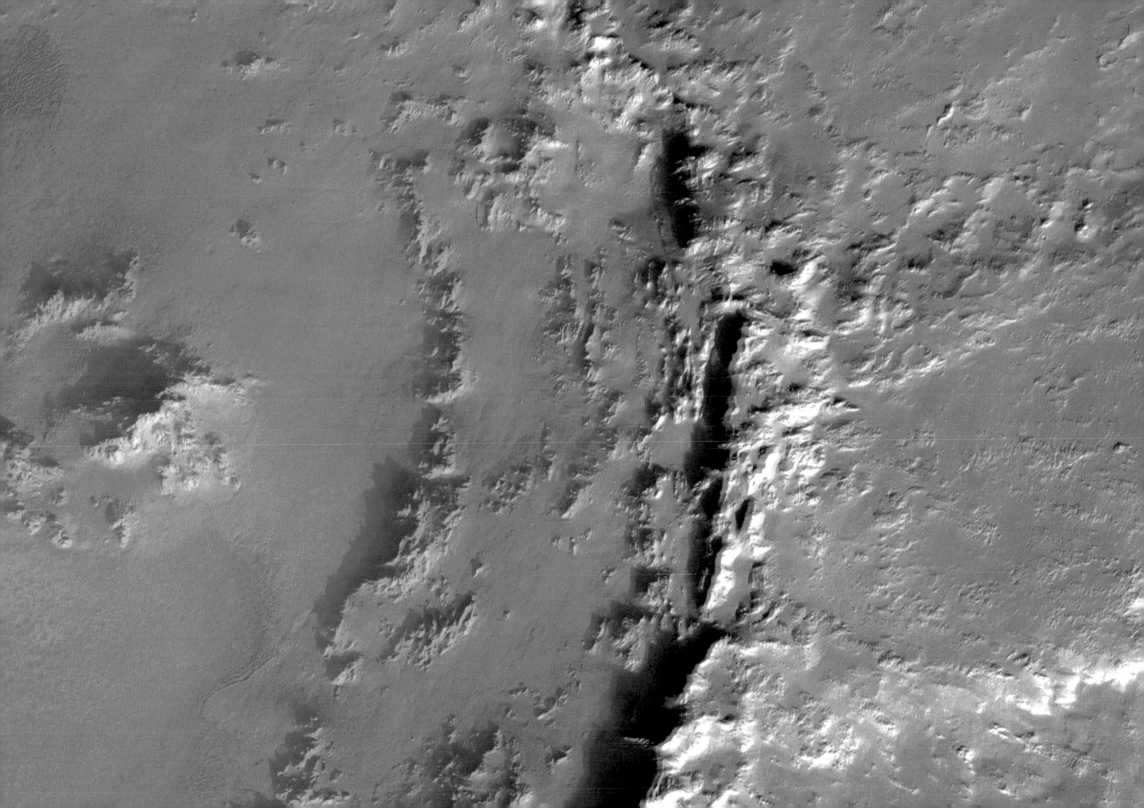

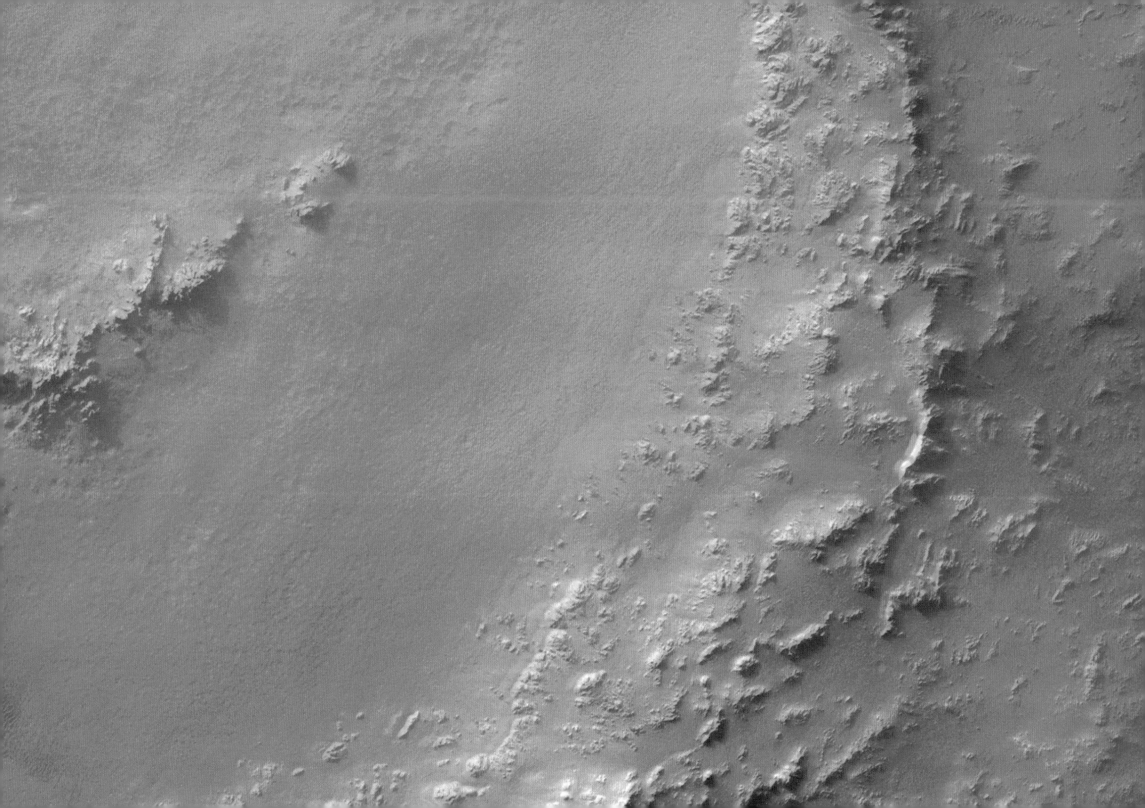

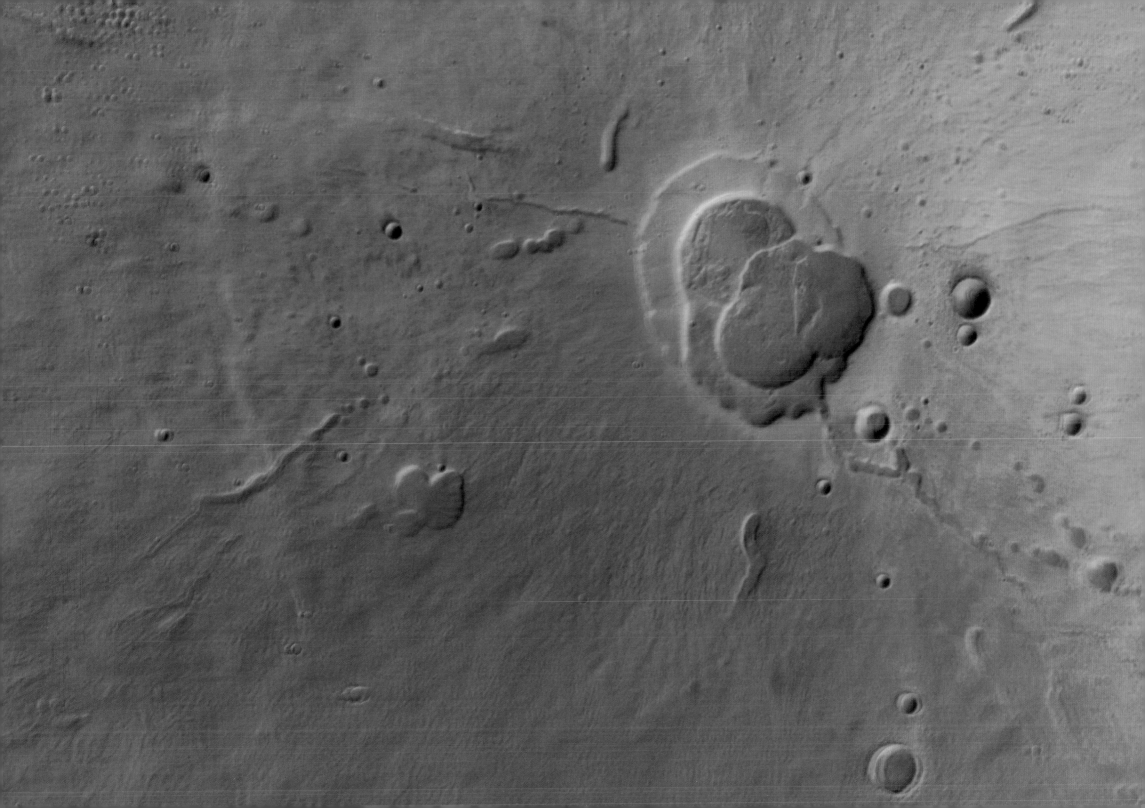

CRATER TERRACES LIKE TREE RINGS

CHAOTIC LANDSCAPES

Left: *the caldera (cauldron-shaped crater) of the Hecates Tholus volcano. Its terraces, falling steeply down from a height of about 600 metres, indicate that the sides of the crater have collapsed several times. Studies of these crater terraces reveal something of the history of the Red Planet, just as tree rings show the age and history of a tree.*

Following pages, left: *this region is aptly named Aureum Chaos. It is composed of rugged highlands, and peculiar-shaped mountains exposed by erosion, which climb high into the skies. Right: the faults, landslides and tectonic trenches visible here are characteristic of the Tithonium Chasma region.*

215

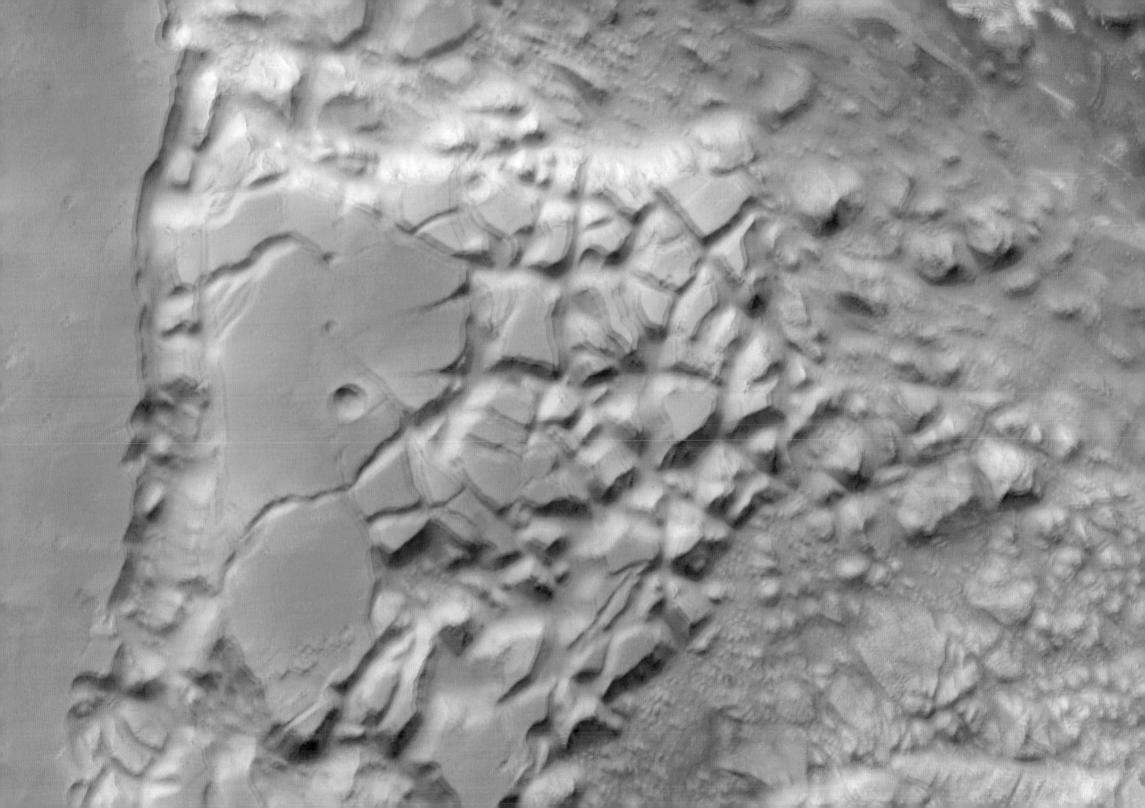

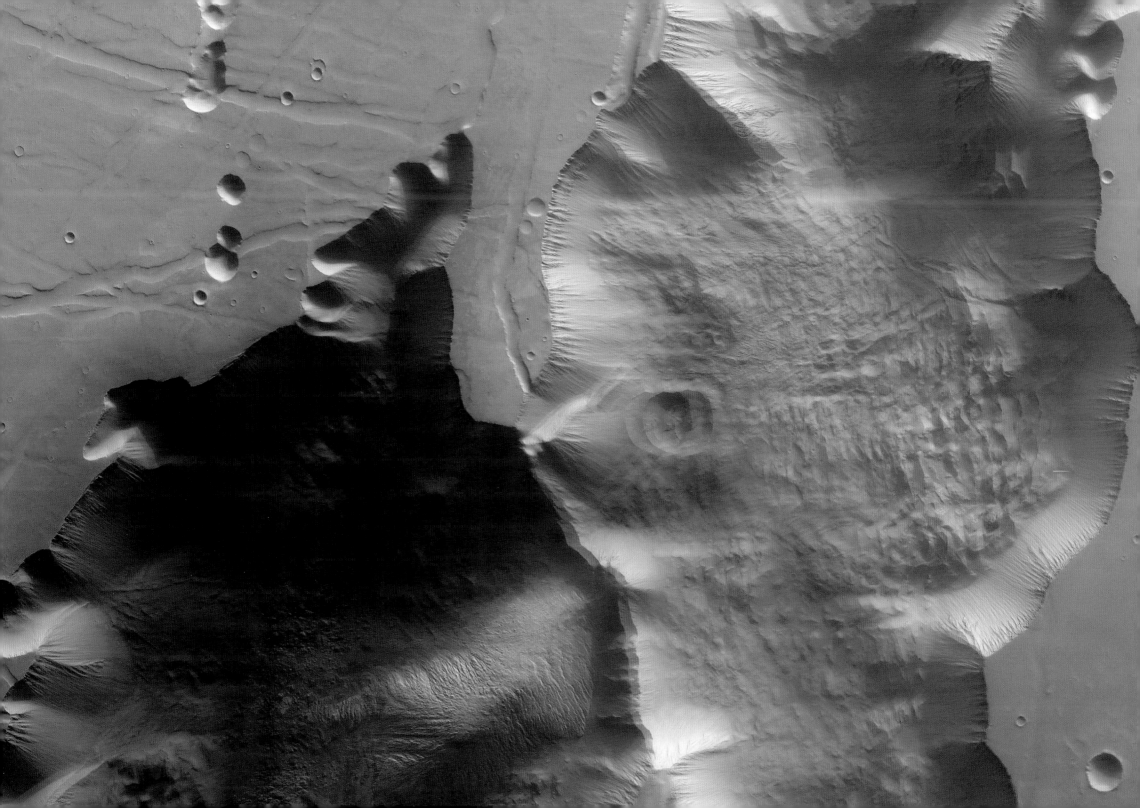

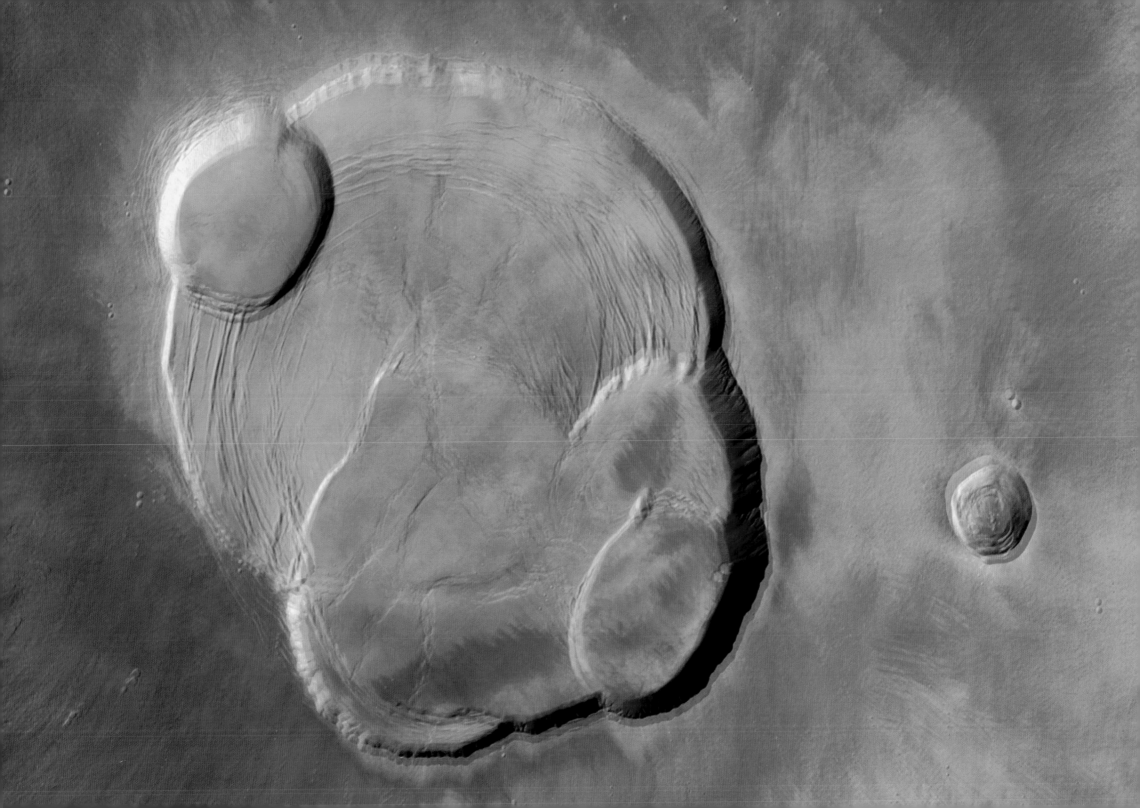

THE EXTINCT GIANT

Left: *view of the crater basin of the long-extinct Olympus Mons volcano. However, much to the surprise of scientists, Mars Express has demonstrated that there may still be volcanic activity at other locations on Mars.*

Following pages, left: *the western flank of Olympus Mons, the most immense volcano in the entire Solar System. The steep slopes shown here rise up to over 7,000 meters above the plain, while the volcano has a total height of more than 20 kilometres.*

Following pages, right: *these unusual depressions are collapsed lava channels around the edge of another volcano.*

219

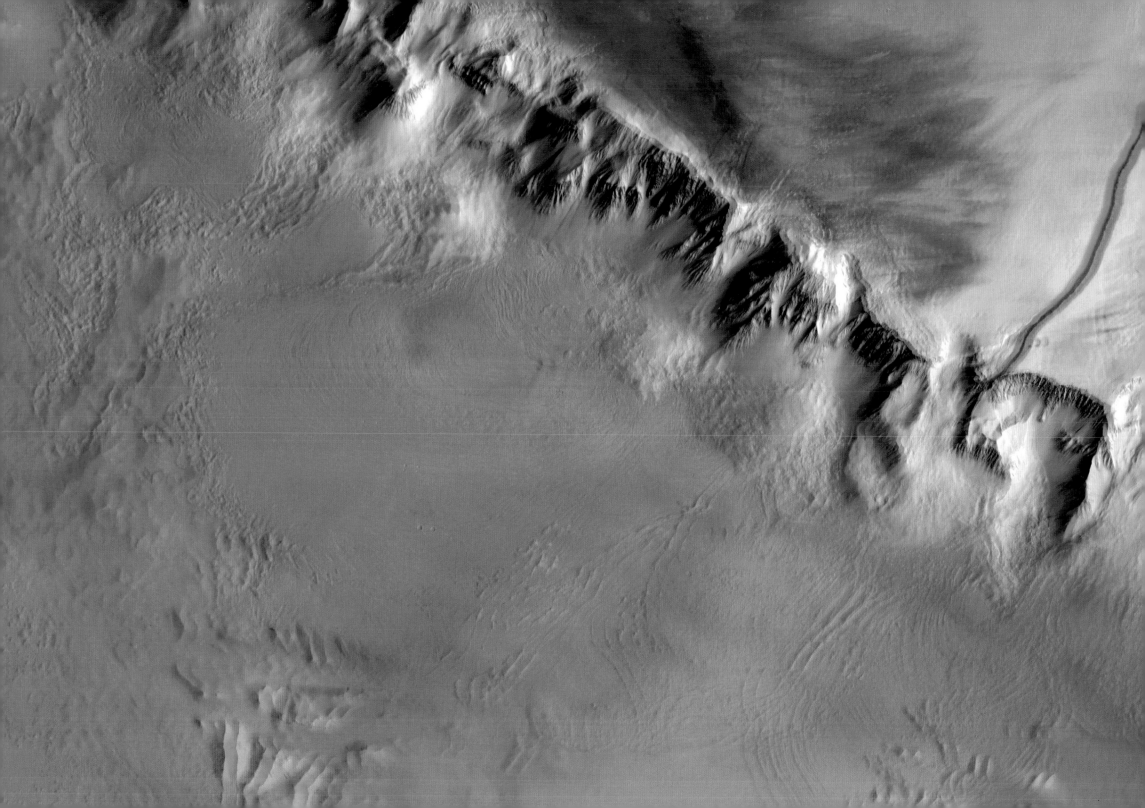

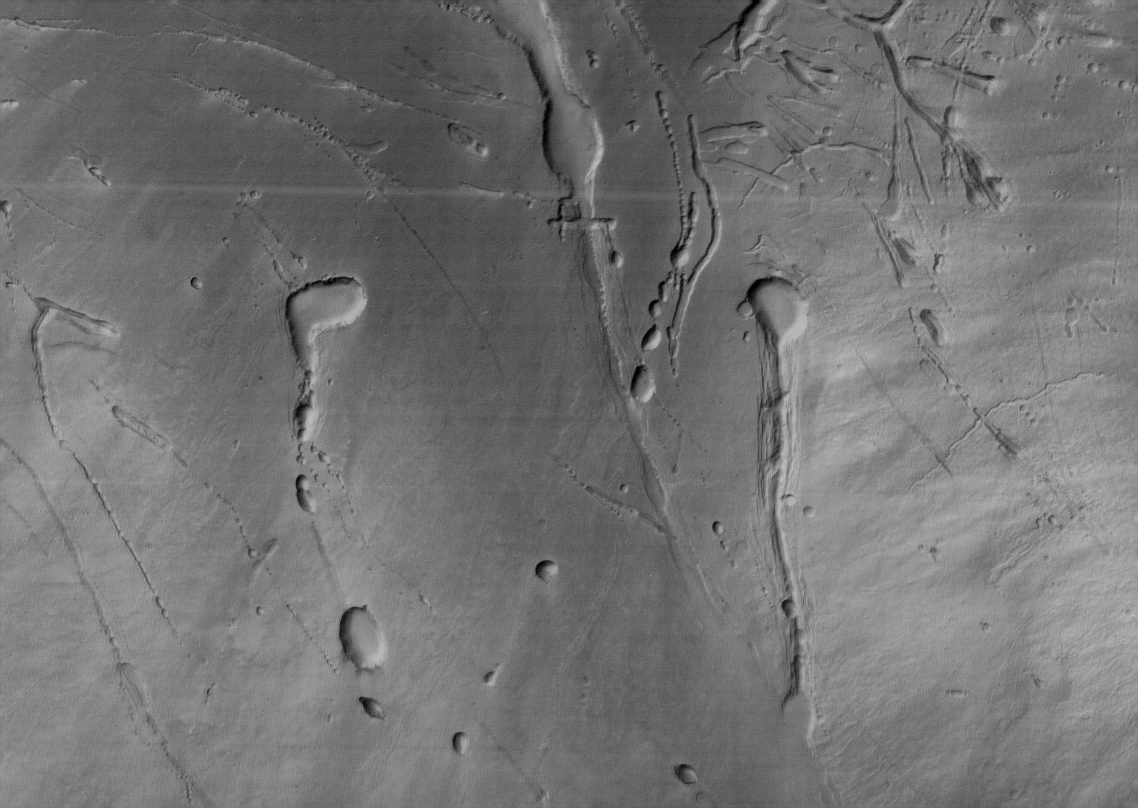

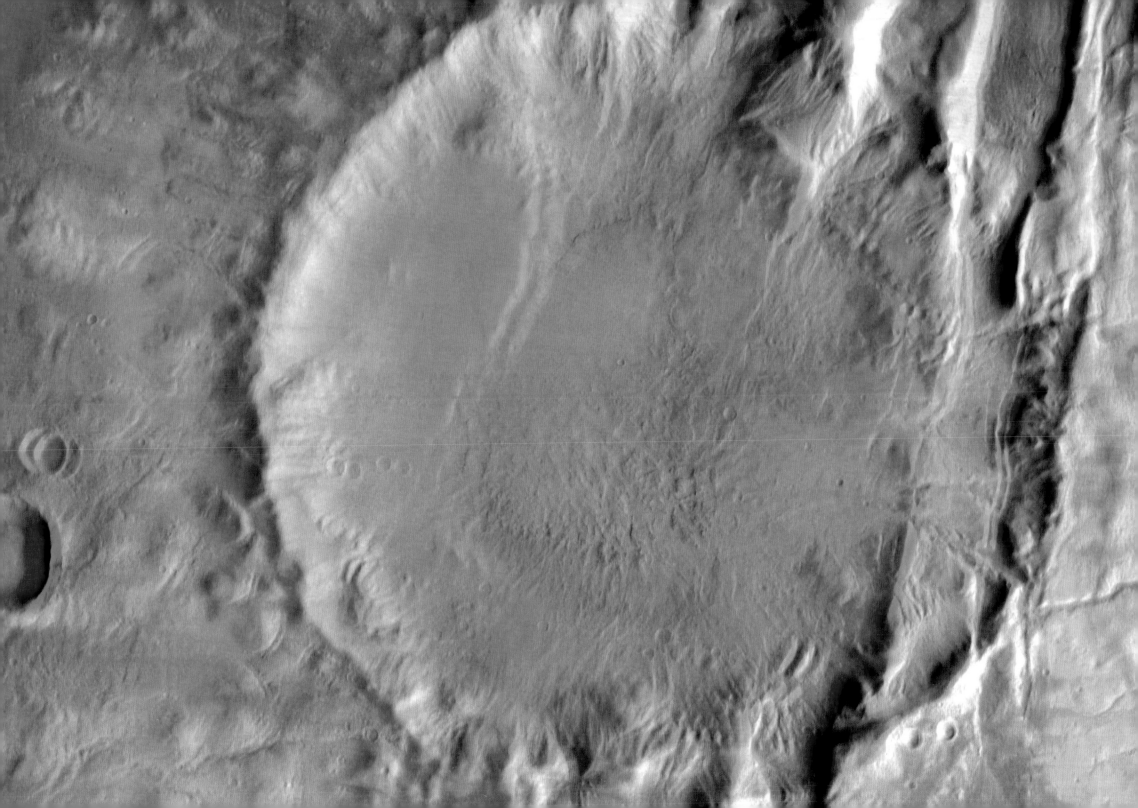

TECTONICS ON MARS

Left: *grooves created by movements in Mars's crust slice across this crater.*

Following pages, left: *the seven-kilometre high cliffs of Candor Chasma. It is still not fully understood how these vast geological structures came to be formed on Mars. One possible explanation is that strains on the Martian crust caused it to fracture and the valley floor to sink.*

Following pages, right: *the landscape of the Claritas Fossae region shows clear signs of strong tectonic activity.*

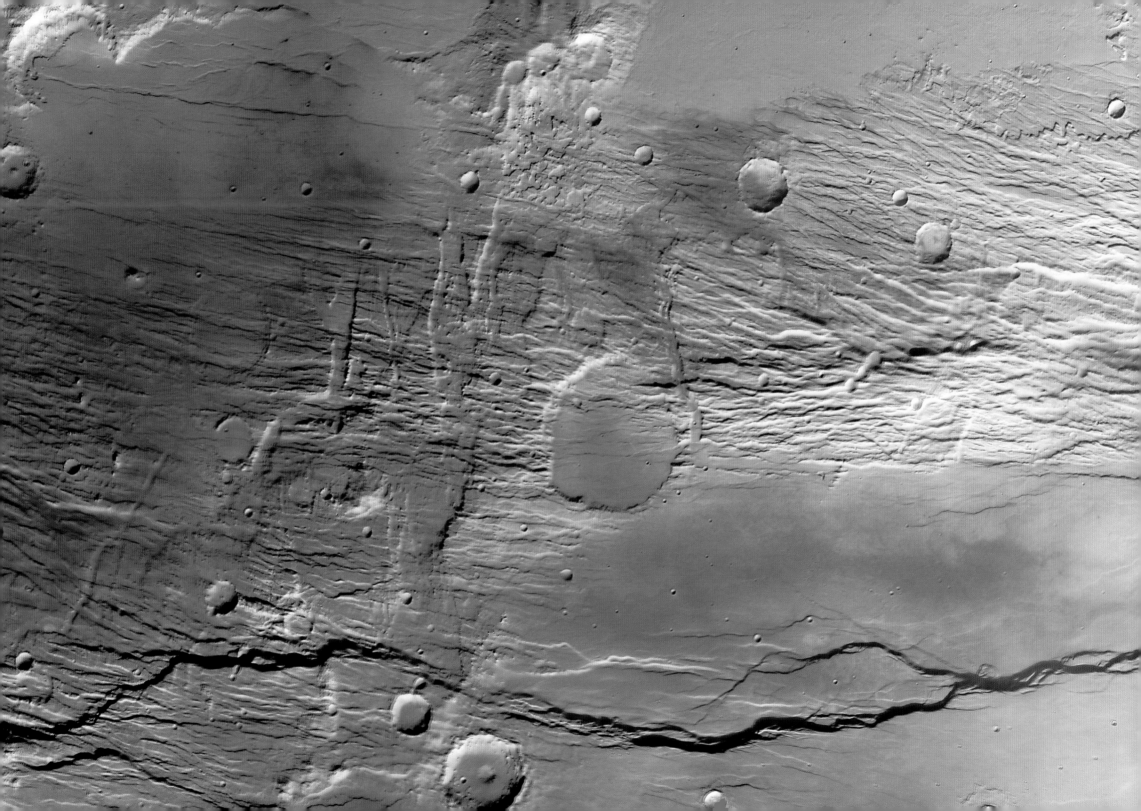

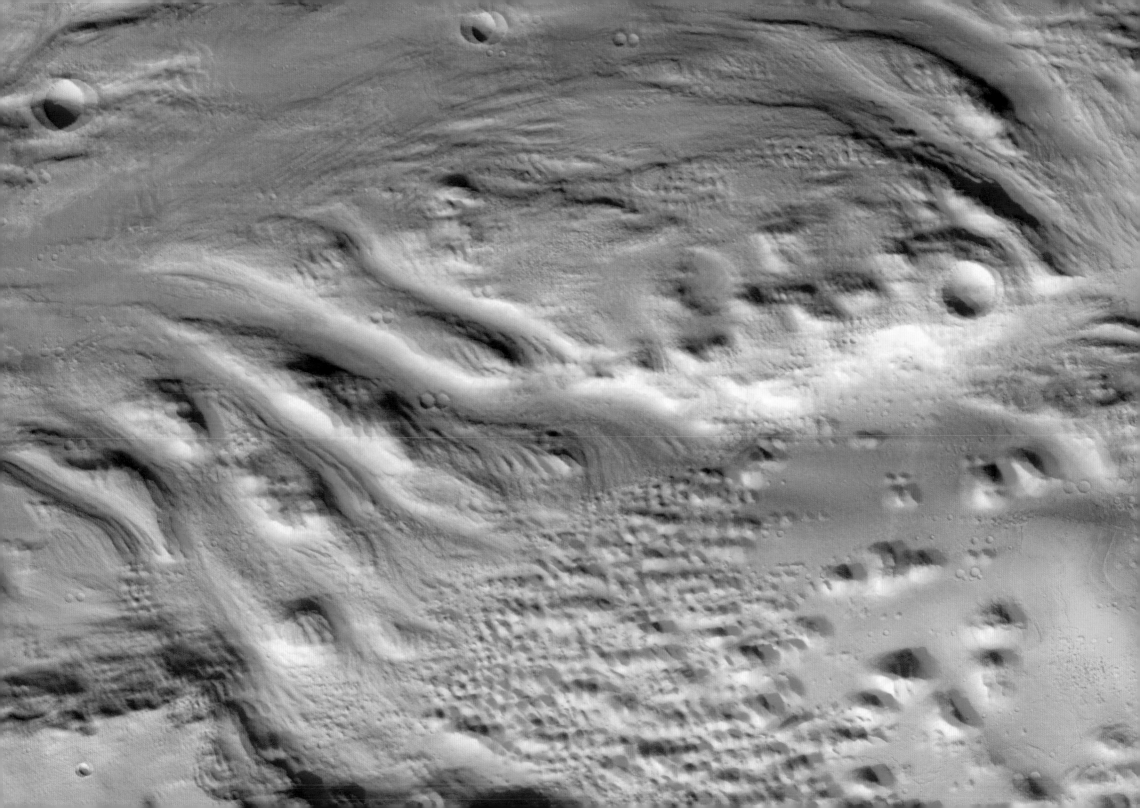

MUCH ADO ABOUT CANALS

TRACES OF WATER

Left: *Ares Valles. This picture clearly shows drain channels through which, at one time, great masses of water must have poured. More than 100 years ago, the suggestion that there could be water and canals on Mars was already giving rise to feverish speculation about life on the planet. In 1877, Italian astronomer Giovanni Schiaparelli believed he had discovered "canali" (canals) on Mars. It was his misleading choice of words that gave rise to all the legends of intelligent civilisations on Mars, thought to be capable of setting up irrigation systems ringing the entire planet. The view that Mars was home to extraterrestrial life has continued to hold sway until recent times. In 1938 American actor and film director Orson Welles caused a veritable furore when he broadcast his radio adaptation of H.G. Wells's "The War of the Worlds", written in 1898. The story, in which Martians take over the Earth, seemed so realistic to listeners that it provoked scenes of panic on America's streets. Today, our image of Mars is a more realistic one. Yet, the search for life – albeit only in primitive form – is still the source of much excitement, and not just among scientists. Indeed, that greatest of puzzles still remains unsolved.*

Double-page spread, overleaf: *this spectacular landscape close to the Martian equator shows clear traces of erosion due to running water that must once have existed on Mars.*

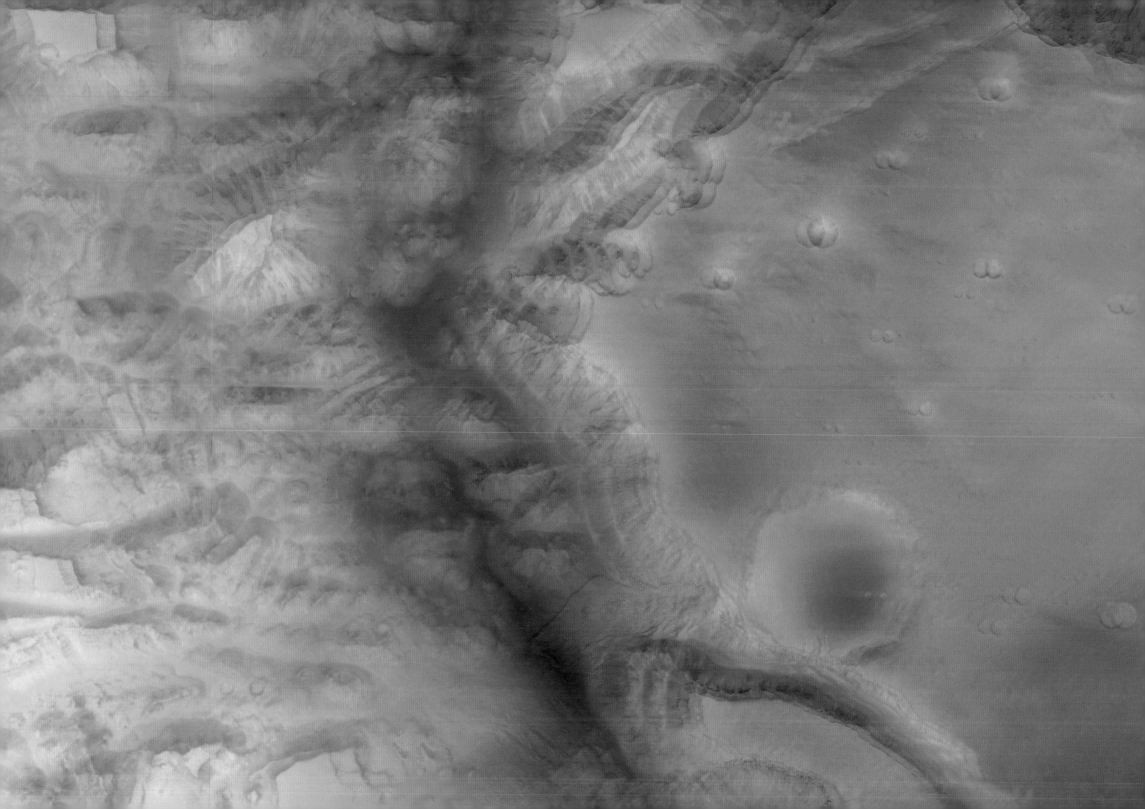

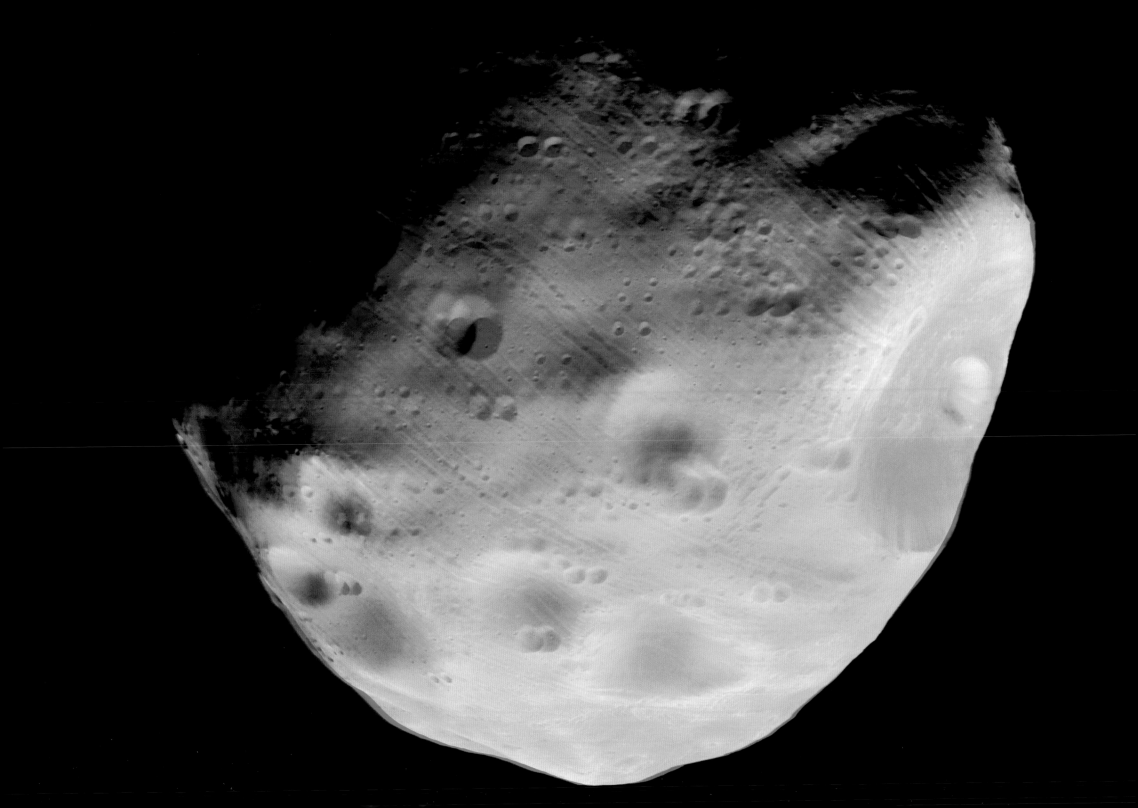

DEATH SPIRAL OF A MOON

MAGNIFICENT DESOLATION

When the High Resolution Stereo Camera (HRSC) set out to take a picture of the Martian moon, Phobos, a mere 20 kilometres or so across, scientists were astonished to find that it was not where it was supposed to be. It transpired that Phobos was faster than had been assumed and was already considerably further along its 6,000 kilometre high orbit. In fact, Phobos is so fast that it orbits the planet twice a day. Yet, in about 50 million years, it will have met its end: travelling faster and faster on an ever tighter trajectory, one day it will, due to the increasing pull of the planet, smash into the surface or instead break apart before doing so. Deimos, on the other hand, the second and even smaller moon, is moving further and further away from Mars and will at some point break free. Incidentally, our Moon, which orbits the Earth at ever greater distances, is also trying to escape our planet's clutches. Thus, at some point in the distant future it will cease to provide the total solar eclipse we are currently able to admire; from the Earth, the Moon will appear too small to fully obscure the Sun.

This picture of Phobos, taken by the HRSC (once the camera had finally caught up with it), shows not only craters but also strange grooves, which have yet to be explained.

"Magnificent desolation" – these were the words Edwin Aldrin used to describe his impressions upon landing on the Moon. Pictures of cratered Martian landscapes can provoke a similar reaction. This peculiar world, so barren and precipitous in aspect, exerts the most powerful fascination upon us, all the more so now that it can be observed from close up in 3D. The following pages contain more "stereo" images taken by the German-made HRSC camera on board ESA's Mars Express probe, showing landscapes, valleys and trenches gouged out by meteorite impacts and a patch of permanent water ice on the floor of a crater. Of particular interest are the last two pictures at the end of this chapter, in which the same region is shown from different perspectives. The first is a 3D image of the Nicholson crater with its imposing central peak, while the image alongside, which also has to be viewed with the 3D glasses, has been converted into an artificial perspective view with the original colours restored – a remarkable achievement both in terms of camera technology and of image processing.

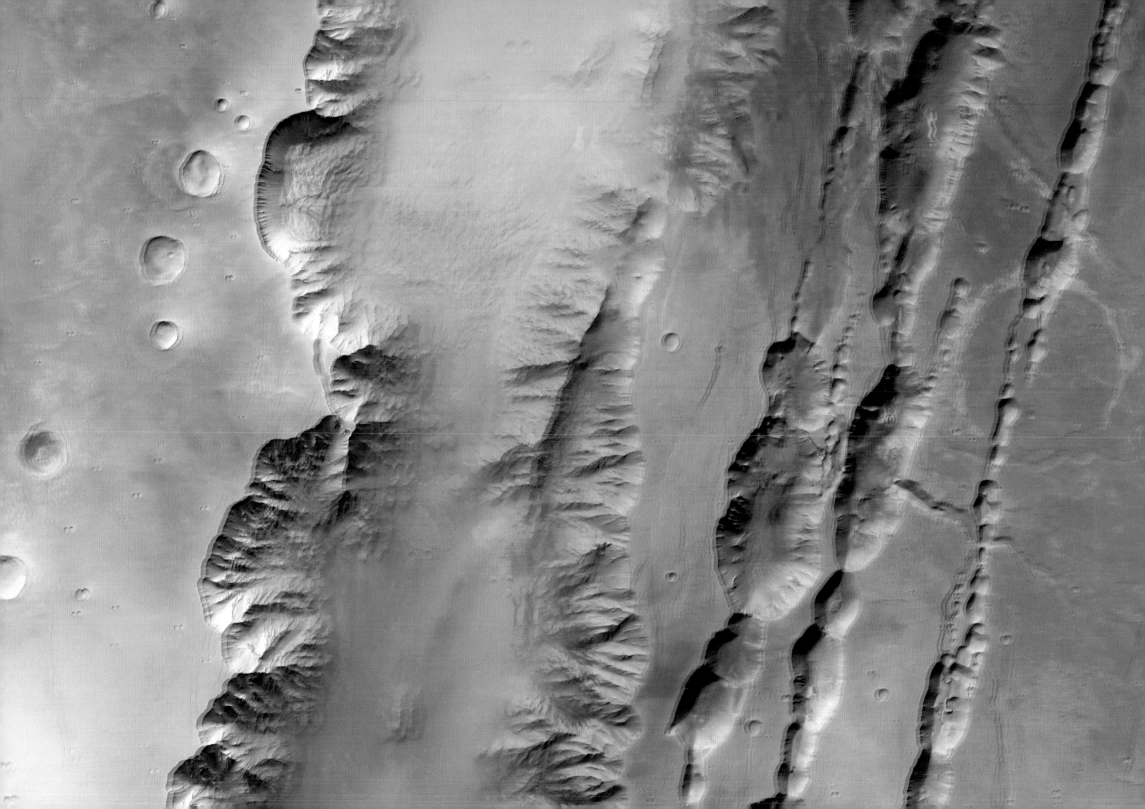

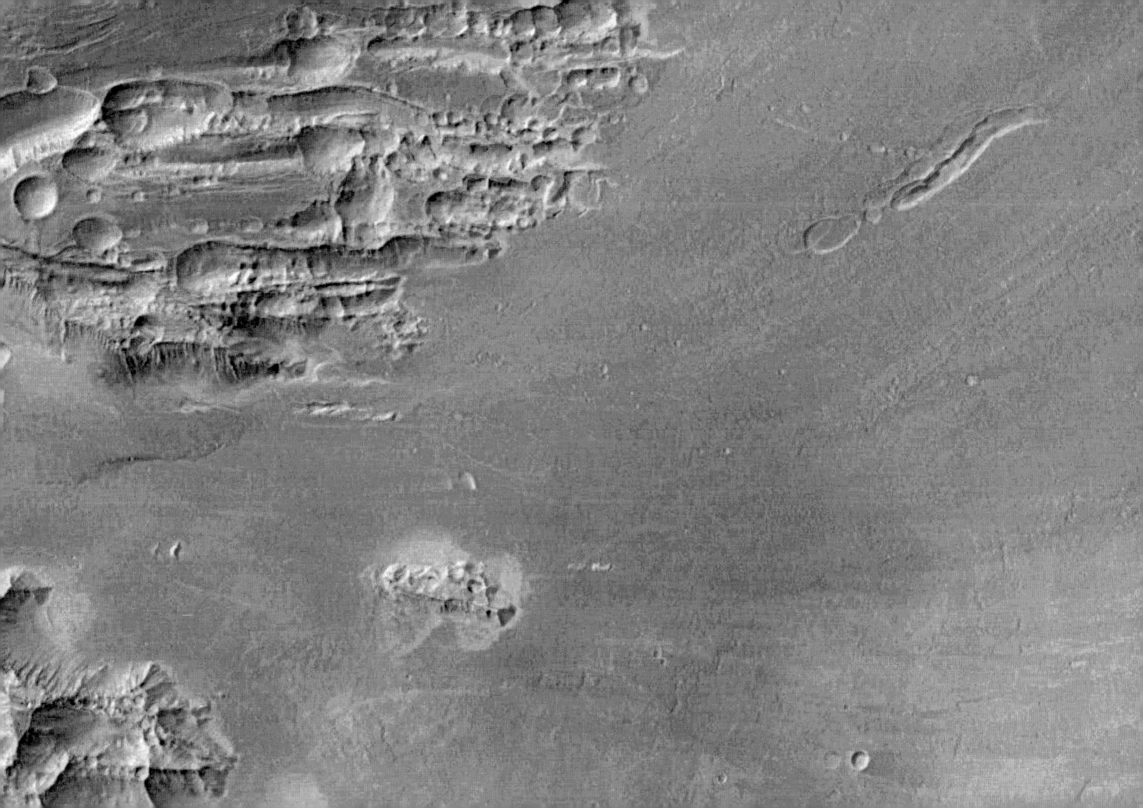

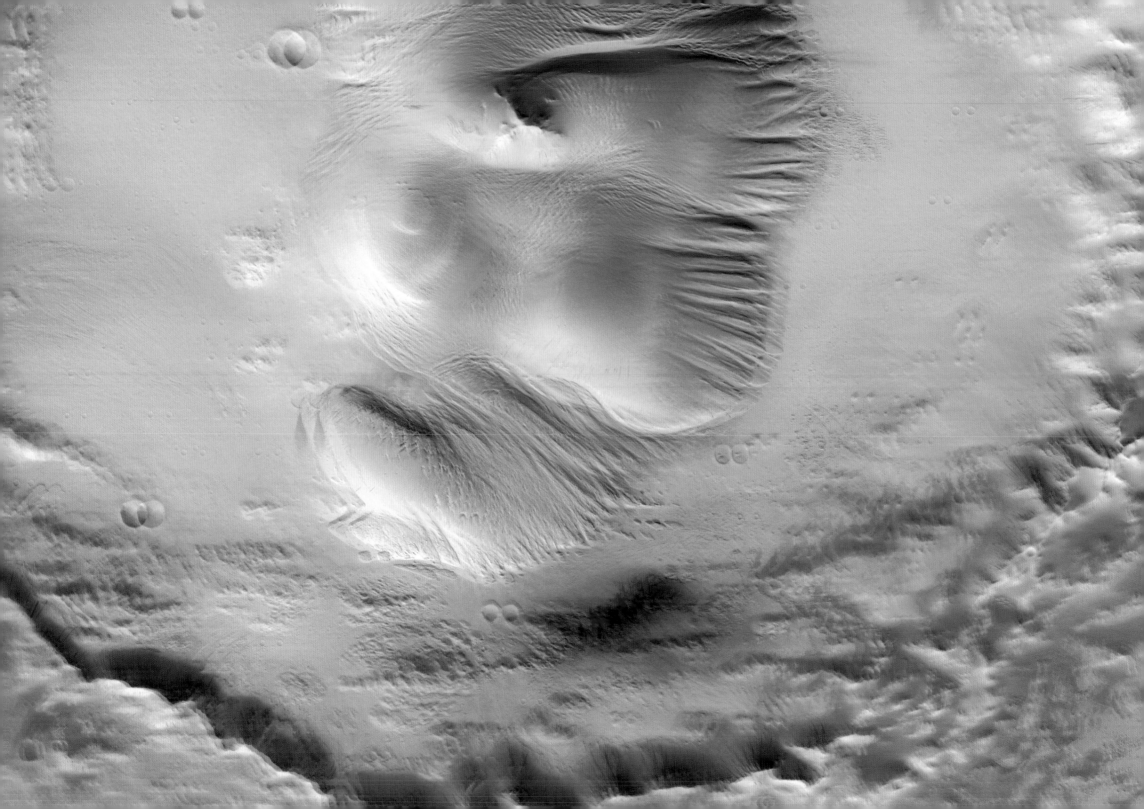

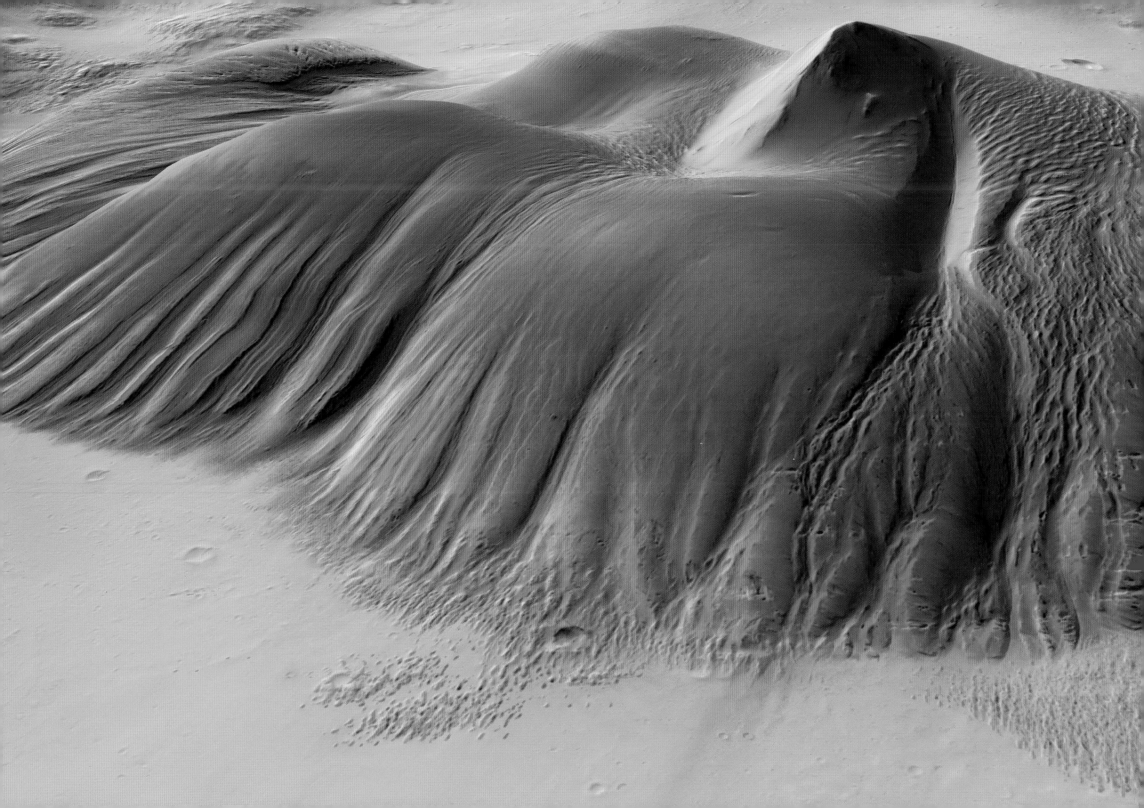

A MAGICAL JOURNEY THROUGH SPACE AND TIME

A MAGICAL JOURNEY THROUGH SPACE AND TIME

The universe and its endless expanses replete with mystery: dying stars, black holes, colliding galaxies. With the use of satellites and probes, we are constantly broadening our horizons: for example, microwave sensors measure background radiation, that mysterious "echo" of the Big Bang still detectable to this day. Infrared telescopes track mysterious distant objects, which only stand out from their surroundings due to their temperature. Some satellites are equipped with "X-ray eyes" designed to locate and examine black holes, while other instruments detect gamma ray bursts from exploding stars. Thus, by investigating the widest range of phenomena, from the coldest objects at the outer reaches of the known universe to the hottest and most violent processes taking place in stars and galaxies, it is hoped that a better understanding will be gained of the composition and development of the cosmos.

The insights obtained in this way are constantly providing answers to fundamental questions on the borderline between natural science and philosophy. For example, are we alone in the universe or do other life forms exist? How did the universe come into being and life become established? What existed at the beginning and how will the universe continue to develop? Will it expand eternally or will it one day collapse in on itself again?

Within a few short years, the joint NASA/ESA project, the Hubble Space Telescope, has revolutionised our understanding of the universe. It has "gazed" into the depths of space up to a distance of 13 billion light years in the visible (meaning those wavelengths visible to the human eye). And since the light from the remotest galaxies we see on these pages had travelled for up to 13 billion years before being captured by the orbiting telescope, by looking at them we are looking into the distant past, going on a magical "journey through time", almost back to the Big Bang. What the Hubble Telescope, along with other American and European satellites, has revealed to us above all is the true magnificence of the universe. The most beautiful of these images are reproduced in the following pages, taking us, with each new picture, gradually further and further away from the Earth and our Solar System.

Left: colliding galaxies. These two galaxies are still orbiting each other, but within a few billion years they will have merged or, to be precise, the larger galaxy (to the left of the picture), will have swallowed up its smaller sister. Astronomers refer to such cases as cannibalism.

COSMIC DIMENSIONS

The Pleiades, also known as the Seven Sisters, are in fact a cluster of well over 3,000 stars. The seven brightest, which give the cluster its name, are visible in the night sky even without a telescope. This is because, in cosmic terms, the Pleiades are not so far away – somewhat more than 400 light years from Earth – and thus are still within our own galaxy, the Milky Way, which has a diameter of about 100,000 light years. The Milky Way is estimated to contain a total of more than 100 billion stars.

Since, in these pages, we always use light years as the unit of measurement for cosmic distance, it may be that a brief explanation is in order: in one second light travels about 300,000 kilometres, which corresponds to a speed of about 1 billion kilometres per hour. Thus, a beam of light needs just over a second to travel from the Moon, located at a distance of barely 400,000 kilometres. Sunlight takes about eight minutes to reach us, with the result that, when we see the Sun slip below the horizon, it actually did so eight minutes earlier, while, in the intervening period, its rays have continued to travel towards us. A whole light year corresponds to about 10 trillion kilometres. This gives some impression of the huge numbers involved, especially since the distances referred to are often in the many millions and even billions of light years. It also explains why scientists generally prefer to use light years: a more readily understandable unit of measurement.

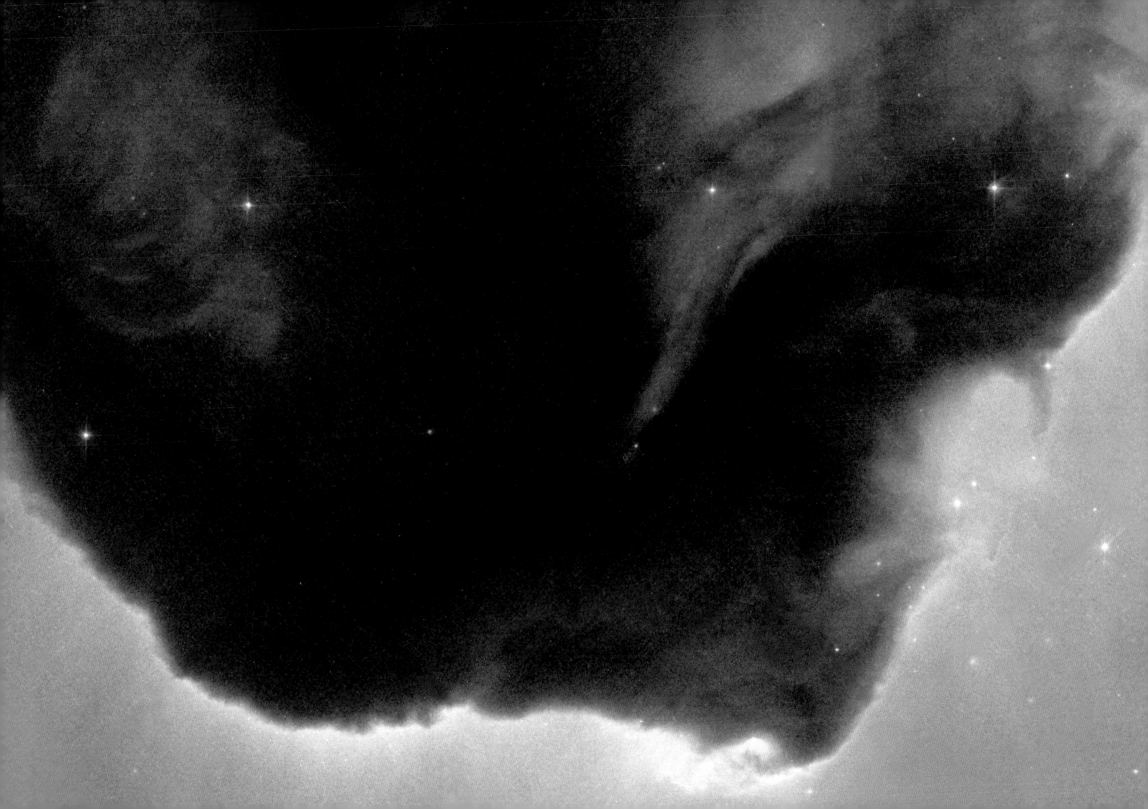

Let us continue on our journey, this time moving further away from the Earth and our Solar System but staying within the Milky Way. If we were able to travel through space at the speed of light (300,000 kilometres per second), it would take us 1,100 years to reach the famous Horsehead Nebula (left) – still almost on our doorstep in astronomical terms. Since probes travel at only a fraction of that speed, such journeys are simply impossible. However, to obtain images such as that on the left, all that is required is to place satellites in orbit only a few hundred kilometres above the Earth. From that vantage point outside the atmosphere, there are no layers of air to interfere with the view. This makes it possible to observe far distant phenomena in greater detail than ever before, such as the birth of a star (main picture, left) as it is formed out of the particles in the dark dust cloud (visible in the top left of the picture).

Right: *the Hubble Telescope orbits the Earth at an altitude of about 600 kilometres. Since coming into operation, it has been repaired and serviced several times. To carry out such tasks, astronauts like ESA's Claude Nicollier of Switzerland (seen here at work) have to exit the Space Shuttle and "capture" the powerful instrument. In the future, it should be possible for robots to carry out such tasks.*

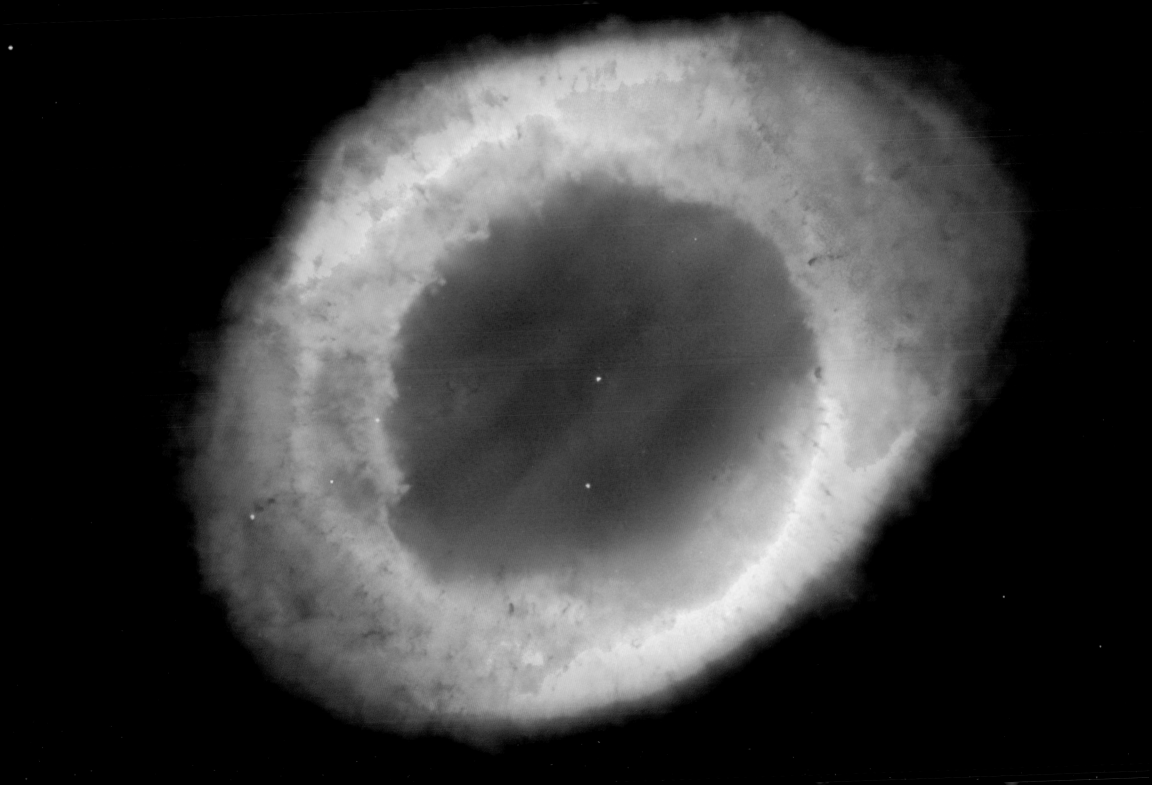

THE LAST GLIMMER FROM A DYING STAR

STRANGE TENDENCY TOWARDS SYMMETRY

*The Ring Nebula (M57), situated some 2,000 light years from Earth.
This splendid structure is in fact the last glimmer from a dying star.
Even suns – which of course are none other than stars – have a limited
life span. When after many billions of years a sun runs out of fuel, the
processes inside it run out of control, causing it to expand massively
one last time until a colossal explosion occurs and most of its matter
is flung out into space. Finally, after contracting to a fraction of its
previous size, it goes on glowing, although by now, it has been transformed into a "white dwarf". The exploded shell of the star, meanwhile,
continues to offer up a magnificently colourful spectacle.*

*The picture below shows another example of a star as it reaches the
end of its "life". M2-9, which is 2,100 light years away, is not unlike our
own Sun. Here it can be seen with its matter streaming out into space,
which is what gives rise to the unusual shape (this effect, like the
contrail of a jet plane, is caused by the high speeds of the emissions).
However, there is still no conclusive answer to the question of why
dying stars frequently display such symmetry.*

247

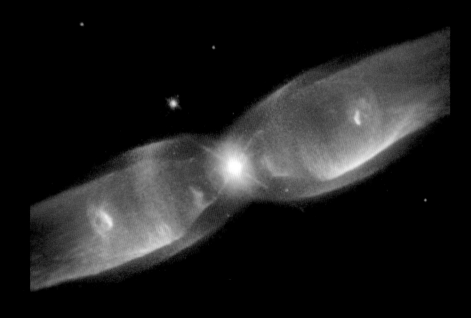

LETHAL BEAUTY: THE CAT'S EYE NEBULA

The Cat's Eye Nebula, some 3,000 light years away. It is one of the most complex and delicate objects among the "planetary nebulae", as the gas clouds expelled by dying stars are known. In about five billion years time, our Sun too will provide us with just such a cosmic spectacle. Far beyond the Earth's orbit, it will then expand and shine brilliantly one last time.

Incidentally, the expression "planetary nebula" is rather misleading. In fact, planets have no role to play whatsoever in the last "convulsions" of suns – that is apart from being swallowed up by the giants as they die.

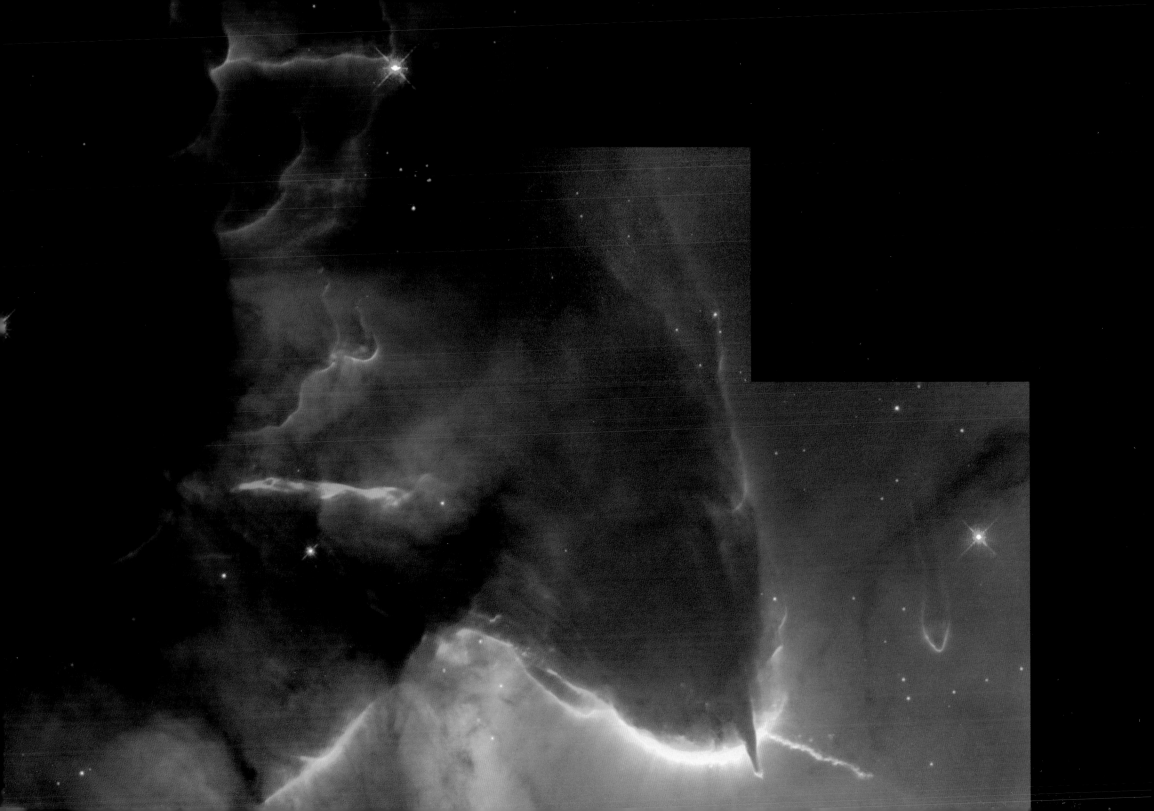

WE ARE ALL CHILDREN OF THE STARS

In the Trifid Nebula in the constellation of Sagittarius, some 5,000 light years away, we can marvel at the birth of stars. The remains of exploded suns are compressed through force of attraction, even when this is quite weak, until a new generation of stars forms from the clouds of gas and dust and a further cycle begins. It was this process which first gave rise to the heavy chemical elements in the universe such as iron, which ultimately served as the building blocks of life. Therefore, we all carry atoms in us that were once formed within stars before being expelled into space. Thus, in a sense, humans can literally be described as "children of the stars".

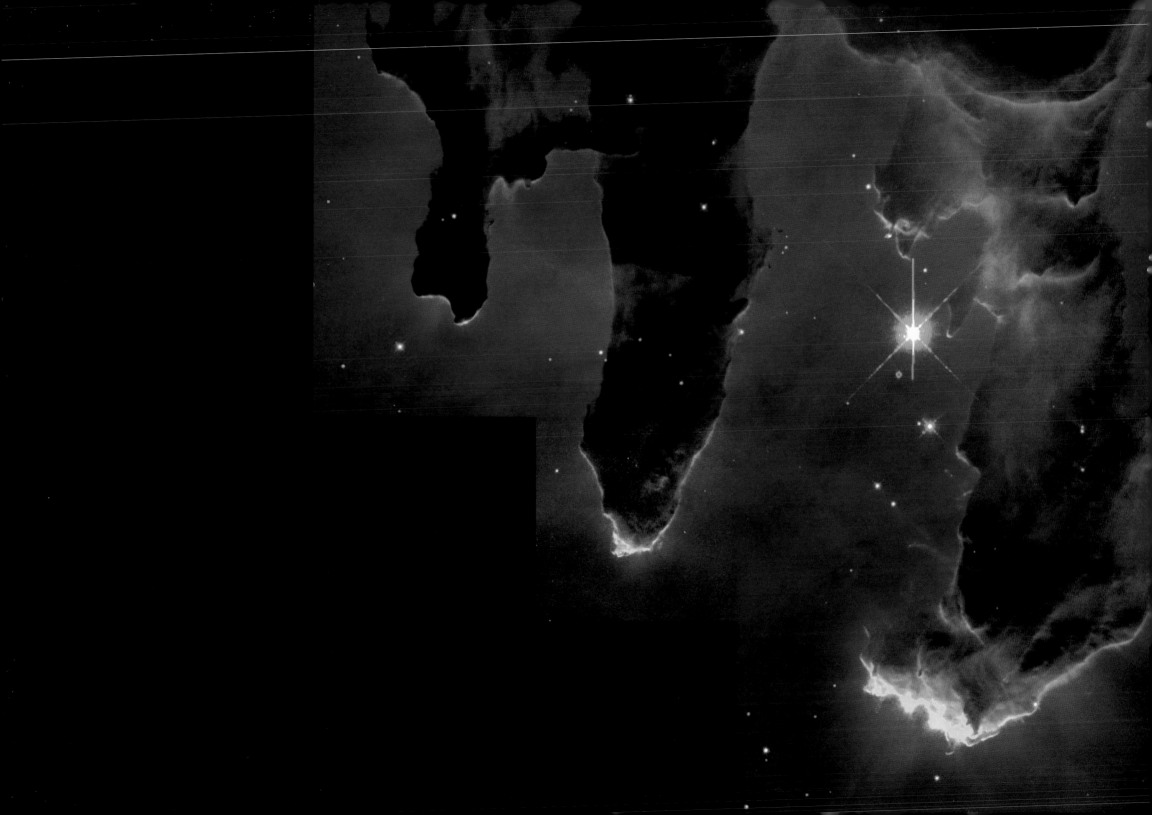

EMBRYONIC STARS AND UNKNOWN PLANETS

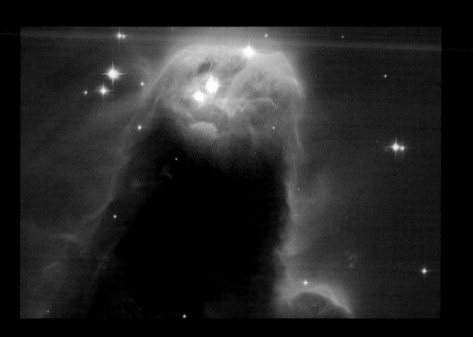

This is one of the most spectacular images to have been provided by the Hubble Space Telescope: although they may look like stalagmites in an underground cave, they are in fact glowing pillars of gas. Here too, in the Eagle Nebula, roughly 7,000 light years away, stars are forming.

The discovery that planets are regularly created when suns are born is very recent. It is only in the last few years that celestial bodies have been discovered outside our Solar System orbiting other suns. As things stand today, in addition to the nine planets in our own Solar System, about 200 planets are known. Whether some are similar to the Earth, and whether they contain any life at all, remains to be seen. Planets are too small for it to be possible, with the instruments currently available, to examine them in any kind of detail from such a great distance. This will have to wait for projects such as Darwin, a flotilla of satellites planned by the European Space Agency, which, flying in a precise constellation, will function as a single giant telescope.

Small picture, right: *the Cone Nebula.*

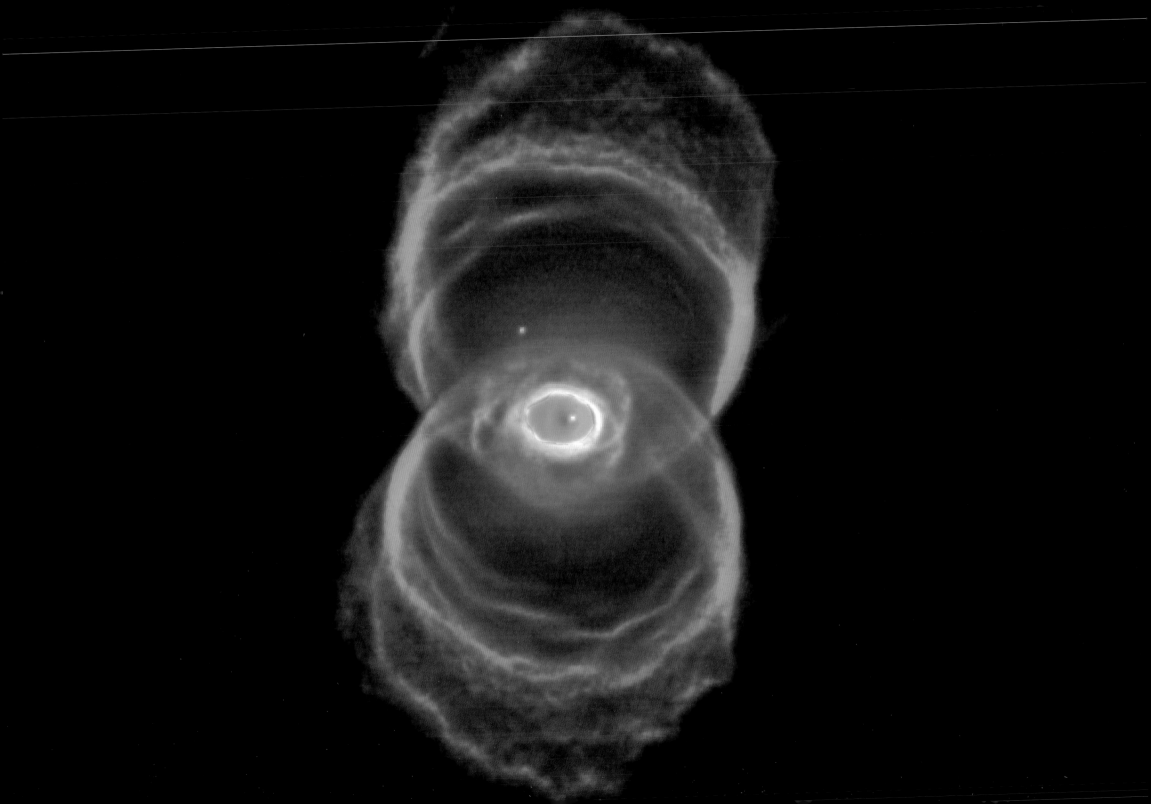

THE ENCHANTING VIEW FROM THE HOURGLASS

*This is possibly one of the most enchanting objects astronomers have
ever set eyes on: from a distance of 8,000 light years, the Hourglass
Nebula (left) appears to be staring straight at us. The eye-like structure
in the centre of this extraordinary formation is in fact a shrunken sun.
The Hourglass Nebula is a relatively young planetary nebula located
within the Milky Way.*

255

A FIREWORK DISPLAY TO END ALL OTHERS

BEYOND THE MILKY WAY

Our Sun is not one of the largest stars; in fact, it is only of average size. The same could not be said of "red giant", Monocerotis V 838. In this peculiar image (left), the gigantic sun can be seen illuminating a cloud of interstellar material.

Some years ago, astronomers looked on in wonder as Monocerotis, which lies in the outer reaches of the Milky Way, emitted an incredible explosion of light (or outburst), briefly making it the brightest object in our galaxy. Since the star is roughly 20,000 light years from Earth, that means that the actual outburst occurred 20,000 years ago. That is how long it took for the light rays to reach Earth before we were finally able to witness the event.

While distances within the Milky Way are already truly vast, they become inconceivably so as soon as one begins examining other galaxies. Apart from a very small galaxy in the process of being swallowed up by the Milky Way, the Large Magellanic Cloud (below), located at a distance of 160,000 light years, is the closest galaxy to our own. It has as its companion the Small Magellanic Cloud (double-page spread, overleaf). Both galaxies were named after the Portuguese seafarer who, in 1519, was the first European to observe them on the legendary circumnavigation of the globe carried out under his command.

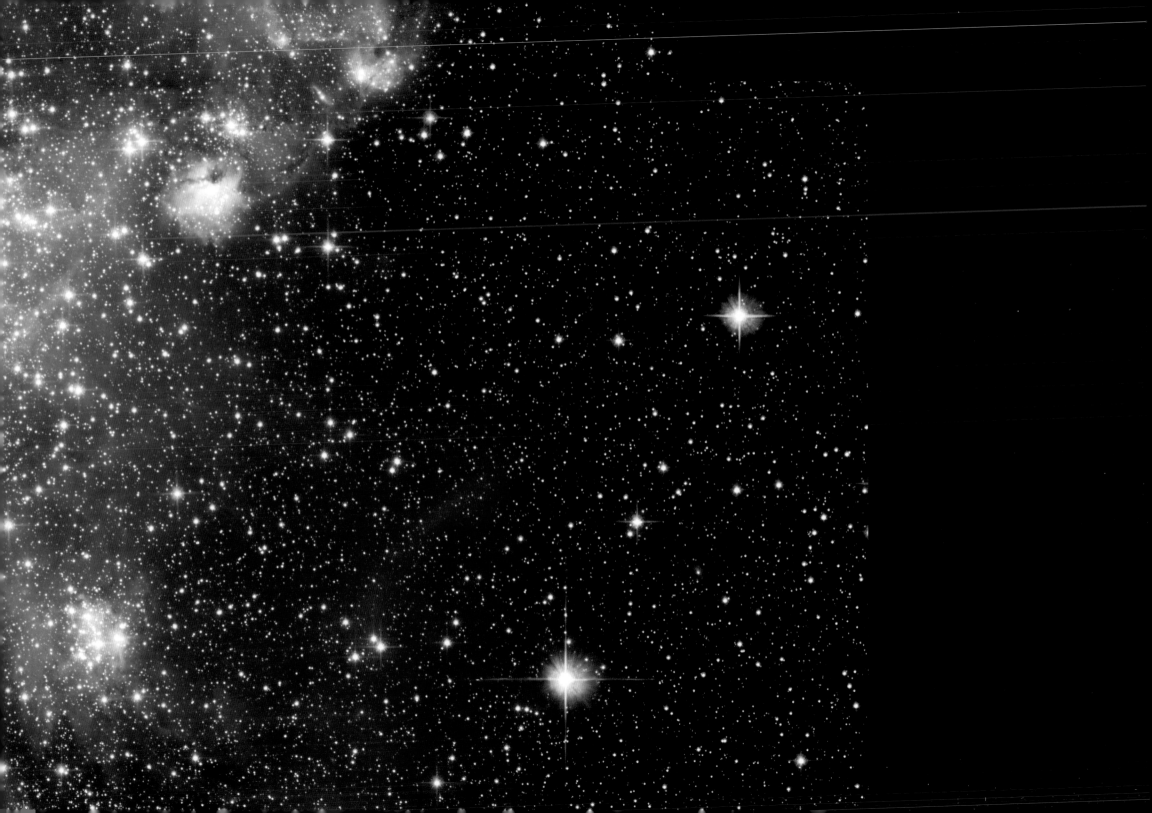

NOT SUCH A PLACID STARRY SKY AFTER ALL

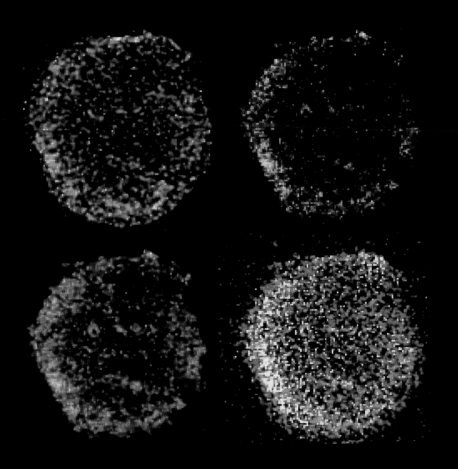

The Centaurus A galaxy (left) is known for the intense X-ray radiation it emits. This radiation is probably triggered by the collision between huge streams of matter and clouds of gas and dust. Satellites whose instruments – unlike the Hubble Telescope or the human eye – are able to "see" highly energetic X-rays have, at a distance of more than 10 million light years, detected gigantic explosions occurring there. The night sky, apparently so placid with its twinkling stars, is in reality anything but. Violent outbursts of matter and of the most inconceivable energy occur every second. If we were to observe the sky with "X-ray eyes", it would be like looking at a firework display.

Right: X-ray imaging of the remains of the Tycho supernova at various wavelengths. The images are from ESA's XMM-Newton satellite, which, along with America's Chandra, can be considered one of the world's most sophisticated X-ray observatories. XMM-Newton's 51 mirrors capture X-ray radiation, thereby revealing a starry sky which is quite invisible to the human eye. The colours indicate the presence of various chemical elements such as iron and sulphur.

RADIANT BEAUTY WITH A DARK SECRET

*80 billion suns make up the Sombrero Galaxy (left), a unique object
which, despite being at the vast distance of 28 million light years from
Earth, is, due to its immense brightness, visible even with simple telescopes as a faint point of light in the night sky.*

*The Sombrero Galaxy's radiant beauty masks a dark secret, recently
unveiled for the first time: at its centre lies a black hole whose mass is
equivalent to a billion suns. With such a huge concentration of mass,
black holes develop such a force of attraction that they "swallow up"
anything that comes near. Even light cannot escape.*

*It is currently assumed that there is a black hole in almost every
galaxy, including in our own Milky Way.*

THE UNIVERSE: PERPETUAL EXPANSION OR COLLAPSE?

*37 million light years from Earth, the spiral arms of the Whirlpool
Galaxy rotate majestically around its centre. M51, to give it its scientific
name, is only one of the inconceivably large number of galaxies in the
universe. In fact, experts estimate the total number of galaxies it
contains at 100 billion. Assuming in turn that each one, like the Milky
Way, consists of about 100 billion suns, it is then possible to estimate
the number of stars in the universe. If one then includes in this truly
astronomical calculation all matter which has not been compressed to
form stars, but which instead occupies space notably in the form of
nebulae, gas clouds and a mysterious substance known as "dark matter",
one obtains a rough idea of just how much mass the universe actually
contains. In the distant future, this order of magnitude will in turn
determine whether the universe can continue to expand endlessly, or
whether the combined attractive force of all celestial bodies and particles
will be powerful enough to gradually slow down and eventually reverse
this expansion. The latest measurements indicate that distant galaxies
are in fact moving further away from us and, surprisingly, that they are
doing so at ever increasing speed. These findings would tend to suggest
that the universe is indeed in a process of perpetual expansion.*

WHEN GALAXIES CROSS PATHS

A GLIMPSE OF THE BEGINNING OF TIME

One could almost be forgiven for mistaking the brilliant white forma-
tion in the middle of this picture for a pearl. What it actually shows,
however, is an immense concentration of suns surrounded by a shim-
mering blue ring of young stars (left), believed to have been formed
when another galaxy crossed paths with this star cluster. As a result,
suns were thrown from their trajectories, and particles and gas clouds
were whirled around and compressed. Gradually, a new kind of order
was established until finally, this colossal ring of interstellar matter,
greater even than the Milky Way, was formed. Since even the smallest
particles are attracted to each other, albeit weakly, this cloud became
increasingly dense until eventually new stars were formed. It is difficult
to imagine a more extraordinarily beautiful spectacle than this, played
out before us at a distance of 300 million light years.

Following pages: *this is the furthest human beings have ever been*
able to see into the depths of the universe. In this image from the
Hubble Space Telescope, one can see galaxies which are roughly 13
billion light years from Earth, and as such are the most distant objects
in space ever photographed. According to current theories, the universe
came into being roughly 15 billion years ago with the Big Bang; this
photograph, therefore, takes us back to a time when the universe was
in its infancy. Thus, what we see here is not these galaxies as they
appear today, since we are only now receiving the light emitted by them
after it has been travelling towards us for 13 billion years. Therefore,
this picture represents not only the furthest ever seen into space but
also a glimpse of the beginning of time.

BROADENING OUR HORIZONS

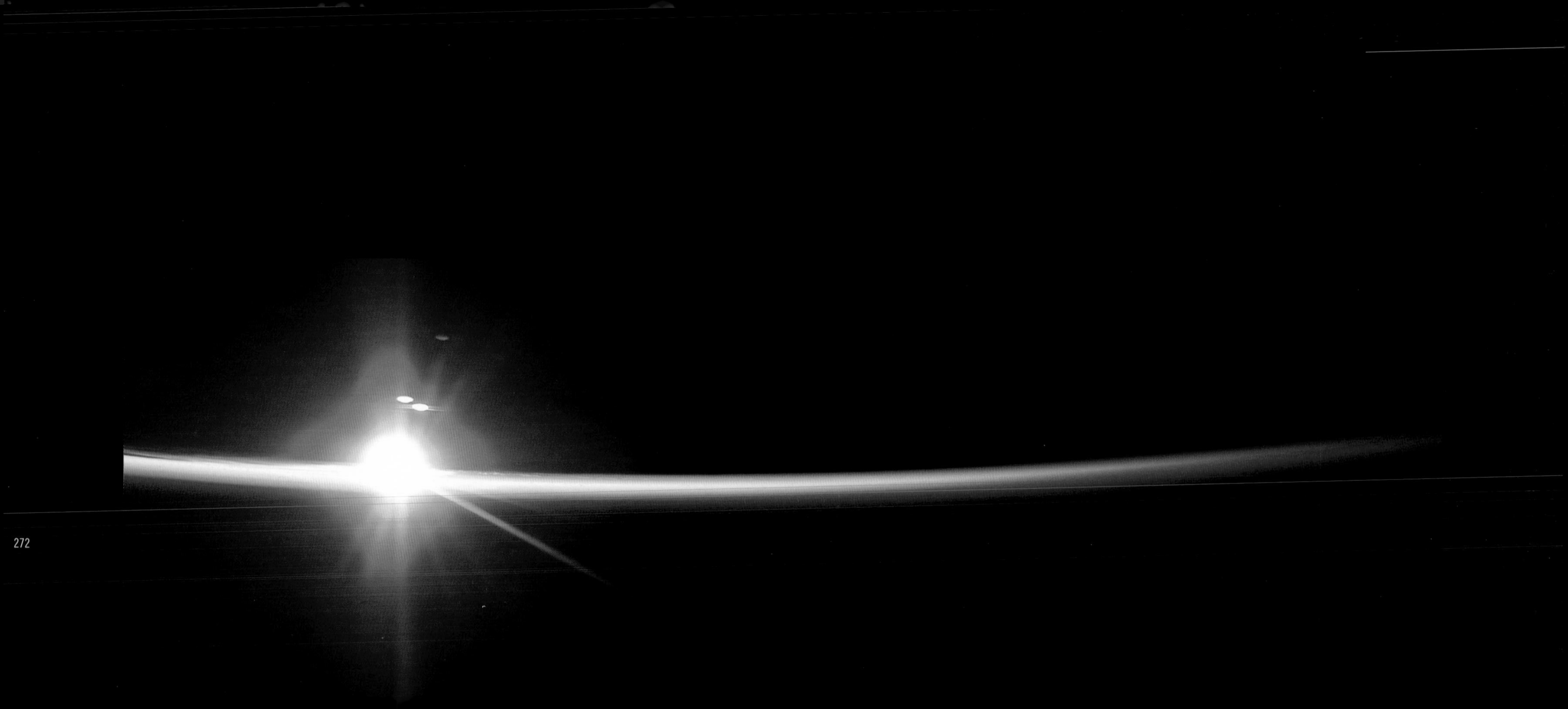

BROADENING OUR HORIZONS

It was thanks to the human space endeavour that our species was able to embark on a voyage away from its home planet for the first time and, in so doing, opened a dramatic new chapter in human history. Humans have succeeded in overcoming gravity and orbiting the Earth. They have explored not only their home planet but also the unknown, distant worlds that lie beyond. What began as a bold vision is now very much a reality – and one with consequences that are far-reaching indeed.

Thus, within a remarkably brief period, space has dramatically altered the way in which we view our world. Take, for example, the data provided by environmental satellites, which, by informing us of the state of the ozone layer and global warming, bring us face to face with the Earth's vulnerability. It also provides us with a far better understanding of many of the processes affecting our planet's biosphere, while reminding us of our responsibility to preserve for future generations the natural conditions on which life on our home planet depends. At the same time, in this age of global communications – yet another achievement of space – we feel closer than ever before to events in even the most remote regions of the Earth. Thus, in many respects

we have experienced a dramatic broadening of our horizons and, in so doing, have allowed a new, global consciousness to emerge.

In addition, we have acquired a clearer understanding of the Earth's place within its cosmic neighbourhood and within the universe as a whole. We continue to explore in ever greater detail our "immediate" neighbours, the Moon, Mars and other celestial bodies in the solar system. We have a better understanding of how they came into being, and are drawing conclusions as to our own cosmic origins. We are already trying to establish whether there are other suns orbited by planets similar to our own. We observe the Milky Way and distant galaxies, gazing deeper into the universe than ever before, almost to the beginning of space and time. Compared with what we know now, the picture we had of our cosmos was, until quite recently, very vague indeed.

And yet, despite all this, we are far from having exhausted all the potential of space. Indeed, it is difficult to see how we ever could, given the fundamentally dynamic nature of technology and research. Each time a new discovery is made, it naturally leads on to further investigations, while for every question answered, another rises to take its place. New applications, meanwhile, are developed in response to the emergence of new technologies.

Currently, even more sophisticated Earth observation satellites are being developed, whose data should be made more quickly and more comprehensively available to service the twin needs of environ-mental research and security. These objectives can only be achieved through continuously improved in-orbit technology and better analytical procedures, such as compatible databases combining to form a worldwide network, easily accessed by those requiring the information, and more effective early warning systems to protect from natural disasters. New, more sophisticated satellite navigation systems are under construction, while in many other ways space is helping to improve quality of life. Finally, in space exploration, the spacefaring nations of the Earth are already turning their attention to what could well be the most ambitious project of all time: the exploration of our Solar System not only by automatic probe but also through human missions. The first objective will be a return to the Moon, followed by missions to Mars, the intention being to first send robots and rovers on reconnoitring missions and then humans themselves. It is hoped that, thereby, conclusive answers will be found to questions of fundamental importance such as the search for extraterrestrial life.

It is with increasing interest that the public follows these plans, which are less about immediate benefits and more about increasing the sum of human knowledge. Thus, space exploration does not merely enrich our lives in a material sense, but also by virtue of the ideals it represents; it is after all one of the greatest human undertakings of our age. We are frequently reminded of its impact on our daily lives, notably when we use applications derived directly from it. Sometimes, however, we are simply moved by its sheer, fascinating beauty, without which the world would be a poorer place indeed.

Images on these pages

Page 272: sunrise in orbit.

Page 275: the Earth bathed in sunlight.

Pages 278/279: a European Ariane 5 launcher during lift-off.

Rear cover: Saturn.

PHOTOGRAPHIC CREDITS:

Front cover: © NASA, ESA, AURA/Caltech, pages 2/3: © ESA, DLR, FU Berlin (G. Neukum); pages 4/5: © NASA, ESA, The Hubble Heritage Team (AURA/STScI). Acknowledgements: Cornell (J. Higdon). STScI (I. Jordan): page 6: © NASA, ESA, STScI, Arizona State University (J. Hester and P. Scowen); page 7: © NASA, ESA, Vanderbilt University (C.R. O'Dell), STScI (M. Meixner and P. McCullough); page 8: © NASA, ESA. page 10: © ESA (S. Corvaja); page 14: © ESA; page 15: © ESA (A. Le Floc'h); pages 16-19: © ESA; page 20: © Eumetsat; page 21: above: © ESA; below: © NASA; pages 22/23: © DLR, NASA; pages 24, 25: © ESA. page 26: © NASA Landsat Project Science Office, USGS National Center for EROS; page 27: © NASA, GSFC, METI, ERSDAC, JAROS, and U.S./Japan; page 28: © ESA; page 29: © NASA, MODIS Rapid Response Team. page 30: © CNES; Distribution: Spot Image, pages 31, 32: © ESA; page 33: above: © NASA (R. Simmon). Space Imaging; below: ESA; pages 34-45: © ESA; page 46: © NASA Landsat Project Science Office. USGS National Center for EROS, pages 47-54: © ESA; pages 56/57: © DLR (Deutsches Fernerkundungsdatenzentrum, DFD); page 60: © ESA; page 61: © NASA; page 62: © ESA, CNES; M. Pedoussaut. page 64: © ESA, NASA; page 65: above: ESA (S. Corvaja); below: © ESA; page 66: © ESA, ASI, Star City; below: © ESA; page 67: above: © ESA, ASI, Star City; below: © ESA, NASA; below: © ESA (S. Corvaja). pages 70/71: © ESA (S. Corvaja); page 72: © NASA; page 73: © NASA (B. Ingalls); page 74: © ESA, CNES; page 75: © NASA; page 76: © ESA, CNES; page 77: © ESA, CNES; pages 78/79: © ESA; page 80: © NASA. page 81: above: © ESA, D. Ducros; below: © NASA; pages 82/83: © EADS, K. Henseler; page 84: © DLR; page 85: above: © NASA; below: © DLR; below: © NASA; page 87: above: © DLR; below: © NASA; below: © DLR. page 88: © NASA, DLR; page 90: © ESA, NASA; page 91: © NASA; page 92: c ESA (S. Corvaja), ASI; page 93: © ESA, Star City; pages 94/95: © NASA Kennedy Space Center; pages 98, 99: © ESA, NASA. pages 100-109: © International Space Station Crew Earth Observations Experiment, Image Science & Analysis Group, NASA Johnson Space Center, pages 110/111: © ESA; pages 112-123: © International Space Station Crew Earth Observations Experiment, Image Science & Analysis Group, NASA Johnson Space Center, page 124: © ESA; pages 125, 126: © International Space Station Crew Earth Observations Experiment, Image Science & Analysis Group, NASA Johnson Space Center; page 127: above: © ESA, below: © International Space Station Crew Earth Observations Experiment, Image Science & Analysis Group, NASA Johnson Space Center; page 128: © ESA; page 129: © International Space Station Crew Earth Observations Experiment, Image Science & Analysis Group, NASA Johnson Space Center, page 130: © ESA, pages 131-141: © International Space Station Crew Earth Observations Experiment, Image Science & Analysis Group, NASA Johnson Space Center, page 144: © ESA, D. Ducros; page 146: © ESA, NASA (SOHO/EIT); page 147: © NASA, Stanford-Lockheed Institute for Space Research, pages 148/149: © ESA, NASA (SOHO/EIT); page 150: © C.J. Hamilton (data: Mariner 10, NASA); page 152: © NASA, JPL; page 153: © ESA, Medialab, page 154: © NASA. page 155: © ESA, J. Huart, pages 156, 157: © NASA, JPL; page 158: © NASA, JPL, FU Berlin (G. Neukum); page 161: © ESA, D. Ducros; pages 162-173: © ESA, DLR, FU Berlin (G. Neukum); page 174: © NASA, JPL, Cornell; page 175: © NASA, JPL, Cornell; USGS; pages 176, 177: © NASA, JPL, Cornell; page 178: © NASA, USGS. page 179: left: © NASA, JPL, DLR; right: © International Space Station Crew Earth Observations Experiment, Image Science & Analysis Group, NASA Johnson Space Center; pages 180, 181: © ESA. page 182: © NASA, JPL, University of Arizona; page 183: © NASA, ESA, Lowell Observatory (J. Spencer); page 184: © NASA, JPL, Science Faction (R. Ressmeyer); page 185: © NASA, ESA, University of Michigan (J.T. Clarke). page 186: © NASA, ESA, Hubble Space Telescope Comet Team, page 187: © NASA, ESA, STScI (H.A. Weaver and T.E. Smith); page 188: © NASA, DLR; page 189: © NASA, JPL, University of Arizona, DLR. page 190: © NASA, ESA, STScI (J.T. Trauger); page 191: © CNES, D. Ducros; page 192: © NASA, JPL; page 193: © NASA, JPL; pages 194, 195: © NASA, JPL, Space Science Institute; page 196: © NASA, JPL, Space Science Institute; page 197: © NASA, JPL, University of Arizona; page 198: © ESA, D. Ducros; page 199: © NASA, JPL, Space Science Institute; pages 200, 201: © ESA, NASA, JPL, University of Arizona, page 202: © C.J. Hamilton (data: NASA, JPL); pages 203, 204/205, 207: © NASA, JPL, pages 208-237: © ESA, DLR, FU Berlin (G. Neukum); page 240: © NASA, ESA, The Hubble Heritage Team (STScI); page 242: © NASA, ESA, AURA/Caltech; page 244: © NASA, ESA, The Hubble Heritage Team (STScI/AURA), NOAO. Acknowledgements: Hubble Heritage PI/STScI (K. Noll); USNO (C. Luginbuhl), Hubble Heritage/STScI (F. Hamilton); page 245: © NASA, ESA, STScI, University of Washington (B. Balick) Universiteit Leiden (V. Icke), Stockholm universitet (G. Mellema); page 246: © NASA, ESA, The Hubble Heritage Team (STScI/AURA). Acknowledgements: Isaac Newton Group of Telescopes, Spain (R. Corradi); page 247: © NASA, ESA, HEIC, The Hubble Heritage Team (STScI/AURA); page 248: © NASA, ESA, STScI, Arizona State University (J. Hester and P. Scowen); page 250: © NASA, ESA, JHU (H. Ford). NASA (Z. Tsvetanov); page 252: © NASA, ESA, STScI, Arizona State University (J. Hester); page 253: © NASA, ESA, STScI UCSC/LO (G. Illingworth), STScI (M. Clampin and G. Hartig), the WFPC2 Science Team; page 254: © NASA, ESA, JPL (R. Sahai and J. Trauger), the ACS Science Team; page 256: © NASA, ESA, STScI (H.E. Bond), page 257: © NASA, ESA, The Hubble Heritage Team (AURA/STScI). Thanks: University of Illinois (Y.-H Chu), Universite de Liège (Y. Naze); pages 258/259: © NASA, ESA/STScI (A. Nota); page 260: © NASA, ESA, STScI (E.J. Schreier); page 261: ESA (D. H. Lumb); page 262: © NASA, ESA, The Hubble Heritage Team (STScI/AURA); page 264: © NASA, ESA, The Hubble Heritage Team (STScI/AURA). Acknowledgements: Caltech (N. Scoville), NOAO (T. Rector); page 266: © NASA, ESA. pages 268/269: © NASA, ESA, The Hubble Heritage Team (STScI/AURA), Cornell (J. Higdon), STScI (I. Jordan), STScI (B. Beckwith). HUDF Team, page 272: © International Space Station Crew Earth Observations Experiment, Image Science & Analysis Group, NASA Johnson Space Center, page 275: © ESA, NASA, pages 278/279: © ESA, CNES. Arianespace (Service Optique Video). Rear cover: © NASA, JPL.

Concept, original text and image selection: Volker Kratzenberg-Annies
Translated from German by Colin McKinney
Picture reseach: Stéphane Corvaja, Nadia Imbert-Vier
Editor, adaptation: Nathalie Chapuis
Art direction, graphic design: Philippe Roure (www.philipperoure.com)
Proofreading: Jonathan Sly

Original title: *L'Espace, les plus belles images*
Copyright © 2005 Éditions de la Martinière, Paris
Published in 2005 bt Harry N. Abrams, Incorporated, New York
10987654321
Abrams is a subsidiary of La Martinière groupe.